Nelson

MW01119609

Harper's New Clothes

A Poetic Critique of Canada's
"New" Government

by Walter J. Belsito
c. 2007

DREAMCATCHER PUBLISHING
Saint John ● New Brunswick ● Canada

First printing, September 2006

TITLE:Harper's New Clothes

DreamCatcher Publishing acknowledges the support of the Province of New Brunswick.

ISBN: 978-0-9739234-5-2

PS8603.E555H37 2007   C811'.6
C2007-900268-4

Cover Design: DougBelding.com

Editor: B. Christian Crouse

Typesetting: J. Gorman

Printed and Bound in Canada

55 Canterbury St, Suite 8
Saint John, NB, E2L 2C6
Canada
Tel: 506-632-4008
 Fax: (506) 632-4009
www.dreamcatcherpublishing.ca

Illustration from back cover: Global Warming Guffaw - Author Mark Tushingham's book *Hotter Than Hell* had the new Harper government grasping to extinguish the novel's nightmare scenario of environmental apocalypse and a consequent U.S.- Canada war over water resources.

*I dedicate this book to
my family.*

*A special thank you to my brother, Larry,
for his unflagging support during the
writing of this book.*

Contents

Difficile est satiram non scribere
It is difficult not to write satire
Juvenal (Satires 1, 29)

Fools are my theme, satire is my song
Lord Byron

Foreword

Enter Canada's "New" Government

January 23, 2006 heralded a pivotal point in the lives of all Canadians. At that time, the author felt concern that the new Prime Minister, Stephen Harper, would subtly and irreparably damage the fibre of what makes Canada such a wonderful and secure country to live in. A year of Conservative leadership and very large doses of neo-conservative ideology have triggered the realization that this was an incorrect assumption. There would, in fact, be absolutely nothing subtle about the changes that would come.

A pre-election Harper had sworn that he would create a new Canada that no one would ever recognize. Sadly, his prediction has become a reality both at home and abroad. The author's writing turned to a previously untried genre - political poetry – that would not only be cathartic, but also would record the actions of a government that seemed to care little for Canada's people.

INTRODUCTION

It is incumbent upon Canadians to not only carefully observe how the nature of democracy in this country is gradually changing, but also to seriously reflect on the cumulative changes that have occurred. Yes, we still have the right to cast our ballots as we see fit and our collective choice unequivocally becomes the reality. However, history has consistently told us that in the workings of a government, small steps lead to giant leaps; then suddenly, a country has radically changed and individual and collective rights as well as the "caring for others" element have been sacrificed on the altar of personal and party ideology.

Tea with the Prime Minister

Stephen Harper is overly obsessed with controlling the press, and with good reason. Many of his actions are very questionable and, thus, would be damaging if scrutinized too closely. Control the message and you control the people. The days of scrums with reporters firing hardball questions at the Prime Minister have long departed. The Harper press conference looks more like a tea party with plenty of cookies to go around for all the hungry journalists who behave. The Prime Minister's Office (PMO) has tight control over who asks the questions. If a reporter wishes to be at the head of the pecking order, the temptation might be to not displease the master. Most in the press corps cringe at this Big Brother infringement of a basic democratic freedom and this country's longstanding right.

Press conferences have become a virtual "cookiewalk" for the Prime Minister, to the point where one feels that he should be paying the television networks for airing what appear to be campaign commercials. A healthy democratic society requires a non-interference policy with the press, for the resultant diversity of opinions disseminated provides the rounded base necessary for an informed decision come election time.

Strauss Lives On and Lies in Ottawa

Stephen Harper's battle with the Parliamentary Press is not happenstance. It is a cold and shrewd strategy that reflects his predilection for the Straussian idea of a 'noble lie,' i.e., those in power know best and, in order to efficiently implement one's ideology and maintain control, the commoner should receive only selective information.[1] Thus, the elimination of the scrum, that wildcard free-for-all that could embarrass a leader and expose information to the public that could detrimentally affect the electorate's perception of the ruling government.

It stands to reason that Harper would prefer to simply and safely send news releases to media offices across the country. This is not new. U.S. President George Bush wallows in this trough of tightly controlled information. In this, the PM has taken on what one describes today as Bush strategy. When the PM makes major announcements, there is often an array of the affected people who have been specifically invited to stand behind him during his presentation. This visual imagery is designed to not only draw upon the viewer's emotions but also convey the message, "*We* all agree with the Prime Minister … Surely *you* must!" The strategy is an insult to one's intelligence.

Imagine this scenario: Hayder Kadhim, the seventeen-year old shooting victim at Dawson College in Montreal, calls a press conference to advocate for the retention and maintenance of the long gun registry. The venue is a large hall for he has invited the families of all those affected by the Dawson College and L'Ecole Polytechnique tragedies as well as the families of police force victims of long gun shootings. There would be standing room only. On second thought, there might be some merit to Harper's approach. The Prime Minister might get the idea that partisanship has no place when it comes to the saving of lives. Police forces have used the registry up to five thousand times a day. Although the initial cost of setting up the programme was very high, maintenance would be relatively small in comparison. Why not keep it? One life saved would make it totally worthwhile, would it not? There are times when one needs to change one's past stance for the betterment of society.

The Medium is the Message

A Need to Know Basis Only; the Less Said, the Better; Party Line Only ... these are all catchphrases of the "new" government. Once in office, the PM quickly prohibited his Cabinet Ministers, other members of his caucus and the government's bureaucrats from releasing any information to the public unless it related to his five-point plan or had been approved by the PMO. Existence of this philosophy flashed front row-and-centre when key government officials were suddenly too busy to testify before a parliamentary committee (the Maher Arar investigation as well as the committee study on the impact of massive Conservative cuts). At the cabinet level during the investigation into Arar's deportation to Syria and subsequent torture, Liberal MP Mark Holland repeatedly asked Public Safety Minister Stockwell Day if he had previously pushed the Prime Minister to fire RCMP Commissioner Giuliano Zaccardelli. Holland even prefaced this question with a request for a "yes or no" answer.[2] Day repeatedly refused to answer the question. This is the transparency of the new Harper era.

One would hope to look to the House of Commons for clarification and direct answers to the questions that need to be asked. The broken record response of "Look at what the previous government did or didn't do!" has become monotonous and extremely frustrating. After one year in office, the government should be doing less finger-pointing and more of answering questions directly and taking more action on the issues that are important to Canadians.

Trail Breaker or Rabble Rouser?

Just prior to the Christmas break, the PM introduced a Senate Reform Bill that called for more public involvement in the selection of Senators. Harper stated that this bill would move the country into a new era in Canadian democracy. Think about that statement for a moment. Here is a Prime Minister who neutralized the votes of the people of Vancouver-Kingsway with the David Emerson floor crossing. Here's a man who appointed the non-elected Michael Fortier to a Senate seat and Cabinet Minister of Public Works, neatly cached away from the watchdog eyes of the opposition MPs. Here's a man who muzzled the press and does not allow his MPs free speech. Here is a PMO that encourages MPs to secretly evaluate their peers. Does this qualify the Prime Minister for the blue ribbon as the custodian of democracy?

One wonders where Harper is going with this bill. Certainly, the appointment of Senators should be more representational. However, a public vote on a list of candidates presented by the PM does not ring the bell of democracy. Here are my three most favourite people. Which one would you like to democratically put in the Senate?

The Senate performs an invaluable check in the end; however, we know Harper's view on checks and balances. It makes good sense to have a body of impartial experienced people (no fears about being re-elected) who provide input that improves legislation and ensures its constitutional legality. They do thorough research, hear the testimonies of appropriate witnesses and offer their amendments to the House of Commons. The Senate does not block legislation. It simply provides a needed second look. Mr. Harper, however, does not like anyone interfering with his agenda. Somewhat oppositional in this respect, his recurring strategy is to condemn the majority of Senators for partisanship in an effort to bully through poorly pre-pared legislation.

If change is in order, each Senator should work independently of her or his political affiliation. No longer would Senators meet and make decisions according to their party ideology. This would put an end to partisanship issues, yet would retain the value of wise and experienced elders.

Harper's aim may ultimately be the elimination of the Senate, which would be a sad loss. More likely though, in line with the PM's frequent glances across the 49th, he may wish to implement a Senate in the style of its U.S. counterpart.

A Cut Below Others or That Dreaded Welfare State!

Prime Minister Harper, when delivering a speech about Canada in the United States, referred to our country as a welfare state in the worst sense of the word. What a tragic opinion of a country that has traditionally cared about others!

Examine the mounting list of social injustices that has grown since Harper's election. Cuts have battered those in our society who need the most help and protection. He scrapped a national childcare programme that was signed, sealed and ready to go and substituted a paltry, taxable $100 month to parents of children five and under. He scrapped the Kelowna Accord, leaving Canada's Aboriginal people impoverished and fighting for their health. He made cuts to the Status of Women and changed their mandate to participation-only excluding advocacy. He archaically removed the word "equality" from women's rights. He closed three quarters of the Status of Women offices and dramatically cut the operating budget. He took away money earmarked for the handicapped, canceled programmes for student work, tampered with money for museums (the protectors of our cultural heritage), canceled the Court Advocacy Programme which protected Charter and Constitutional rights, and killed EnerGuide that gave the economically hard-pressed the ability to reduce their heating bills while helping the environment. This is only a partial list.

All of these cuts were made in spite of the $13 billion surplus that greeted him when he took office. Further, he committed all interest saved from the pay down of the national debt to giving tax rebates instead of developing programmes that would help those in need. What further cuts will come as a result of this commitment? Look south of our border, and then decide which approach to social justice best fits your vision of Canada.

Dark Ages Pride: A Dinosaur Mentality

Mr. Harper questions the validity of the global warming issue. The Kyoto Protocol and consequently Canada's reputation abroad have been compromised by the Conservative's slaphappy and dangerous approach to environmental issues.

Their Clean Air Act, which lacks short and medium term objectives, typifies their egotistical approach to things that already exist: If we didn't make it, we don't want it! The Environmental Protection Act, with some modification, could have been used almost immediately to affect changes that would help the country meet her Kyoto objectives. Instead, there will be a time lag between the passing of the new act and needed environmental action. Most environmental programmes were summarily eliminated and replaced with a tax credit for transit users - a relatively ineffective programme in terms of greenhouse gas reduction. Environmentalists across the world and Canada condemned the Conservatives' approach as shortsighted and dangerous to the survival of our planet. They have recently promoted the future use of ethanol; however, the overall value of this programme in terms of greenhouse gas reduction is questionable.

The government recently rejected the U.S. invitation to develop the Mars surface rover. What a missed opportunity! The Canadarm, one of the country's outstanding advances in space engineering, established Canada as an international leader in robotics. This quick, poorly thought-out decision keeps Canada from the waves of the future and will lead to a brain drain of experts from Canada's space agency. Is this not one more example of a Stephen Harper ideological blunder? Is he afraid of being part of a discovery mission that infringes on God's turf? Surely, one's faith is greater than that.

With this government, it would be an exercise in futility to call for the modernization of Canada's stem cell legislation to legalize researchers' efforts to find cures for debilitating and fatal illnesses. Our country will be left far behind in the dust.

A Foreign Foreign Policy

Canada's foreign policy raises many eyebrows. Most Canadians believe Israel and Lebanon have the right to coexist, and many were appalled when Harper labeled the 2006 Israeli military response as "measured." Canadians have come to expect the government to serve as a mediator between warring groups and realize that a one-sided approach is counterproductive to diplomatic solutions.

Most Canadians prefer the approach of 1957 Nobel Peace Prize winner, former Prime Minister Lester B. Pearson. During the Presentation Speech, Gunnar Jahn, chair of the Nobel Committee, awarded the Prize to "...the man Lester Pearson because of his personal qualities - the powerful initiative, strength, and perseverance he has displayed in attempting to prevent or limit war operations and to restore peace in situations where quick, tactful, and wise action has been necessary to prevent unrest from spreading and developing into a worldwide conflagration."[3]   Harper's support for the U.S. invasion of Iraq, his failure to serve as an "honest broker" for peace in the Israel/Lebanon conflict and his decision not to allow a truly democratic debate on Canada's changed mission in Afghanistan certainly place him, and consequently the country, in a radically different category than Pearson and the "old Canada."

Mr. Harper's Chinese fiasco also illustrated a lack of experience and understanding of the importance of 'face' in Eastern culture. To publicly censure China for its human rights abuses and then hope to affect change through diplomacy was sheer nonsense. Harper's attempt to meet with President Hu is analogous to a high school student who, unfamiliar with the dating process, loudly insults the girl, then in the same breath invites her to the prom. No wonder the PM was left out in the cold!

Harper, in the tradition of Brian Mulroney, has aligned himself too closely with the United States. The Softwood Billion Dollar Giveaway Show with game host S.J.H. emphatically demonstrates the evolving "cozy cozy" alignment with our southern neighbors that most Canadians vehemently oppose.

The Great Divide

The Prime Minister has an uncanny way of encouraging divisiveness. As a result of his failed promise to solve fiscal imbalance, he has pitted province against province. By reintroducing the same gender marriage issue into parliament, he pitted traditionalists against gay/lesbians and those who stand behind their Charter rights. Through his farcical Afghanistan debate and his stance that to ask questions about Canada's involvement in Afghanistan demonstrates a lack of support for our soldiers, he has again divided our nation. Through his "Québec as a Nation" motion in the Commons, he has stirred up the separatism debate.

Consider his new tax credit that gives money back to families with children in organized sports. Granted, hockey equipment is very expensive. However, if this is the plan, then also give money to families who cannot afford to put their children in sports programmes. Don't reward the relatively well-off, and then ignore the impoverished. That comes across as mean-spirited. And what about parents who put their children into arts programmes? Should they be left out? Aren't Harper's tax breaks simply a vote-mongering action that attempts to increase the base of voters who will provide him with a majority government?

The defection of Liberal MP Wagid Kahan and Liberal worker Mark Persaud to the Conservative Party made for a perfect photo op in Mississauga. As Prime Minister Harper stood proudly in the background, Persaud strongly intimated that the Liberals were not respectful of new immigrants. The Tories milked a floor crossing to its fullest. One can assume that the objective of the press conference in Mississauga was to counter criticism leveled at Harper by the Lebanese Canadians for his "measured response" comment during the recent Lebanon/Israel conflict. Unfortunately, the possible spin-off from this tactic is the potential alienation of the Muslim community by implying that the Liberals are disrespectful of this sector. This unsubstantiated suggestion can only do harm to a country that respects all religious beliefs and ethnic groups. Surely, the PM wouldn't sacrifice unity for broadening his electoral base!

Diving Technique 101

Prime Minister Harper has a knack of doing a "reverse twist" when criticized. For example, he will say things like, 'if you disagree with our two year extension in Afghanistan, you do not support our soldiers', or, 'if you don't support the cuts we are making, then you believe in wasting taxpayers hard-earned money', or, 'if you don't support our Clean Air Act, you believe in allowing mercury to destroy the health of Canadians.' This technique takes the focus off of a very often valid criticism and attempts to replace it with an unsubstantiated negative attributed to the person or group who dared to question his decision. We support our soldiers; we agree that tax dollars are needed to maintain important social programmes as well as to control toxic substances in our environment.

The Conservatives did not meet their promise of reduced hospital wait times. At a photo op announcement at Toronto's Sick Kids

Hospital, the PM, with his sidekick Health Minister Clement in tow, announced federal funding of a Canada-wide 2.6 million dollar project. Sixteen pediatric hospitals initiated the study that will monitor wait times for pediatric surgery. Ontario's Intergovernmental Affairs Minister Marie Bountrogianni said Harper should be ashamed about his failure to consult with the provinces prior to this announcement. It seems obvious why he did not forewarn the province about this event. The PM certainly wouldn't want a provincial government member sharing in his glorious moment, even though it is the provinces who are responsible for wait times. The Minister added that the amount of money was insignificant and paled in comparison to the $611 million that the Ontario government has spent over the last two years to reduce wait times. NDP MP Olivia Chow said the wait time situation called for an immediate increase in the number of health care workers. Harper scores a 9.3 for effort, but a failing grade for degree of difficulty for this double twist dive.

Shuffling a Marked Deck

The usual rationale behind a Cabinet Minister shuffle is to refocus the electorate's attention from a bad situation to a fresh start, thanks to the appointment of a new face to a given portfolio. Canadians realize, however, that Stephen Harper controls every decision made in his governance. He is a superb strategist who keeps all unwanted variables in check. As a result, this strategy of Cabinet change is relatively ineffective. Harper calls the shots. When a Cabinet Minister fails, it is unequivocally the Prime Minister who is behind the failure. His only other option would be to apologize for a bungled act. This is very unlikely to happen.

Harper's New Clothes

In the fable, "The Emperor's New Clothes," two thieves convince a vain king to purchase a suit of the finest cloth. The material, they say, has a very special quality. People who cannot see the clothes are either too stupid or unworthy of their position in life. The king, who is greatly impressed by his new suit, immediately puts it on and proudly strides through the town. The townspeople, in absolute awe of the magnificence of these invisible rich threads, were praising the king's own magnificence when an innocent child, in utter amazement, cries out, "He has nothing on!" Immediately, the word spreads that the king is not wearing any clothes. The moral of the story? There is no such thing as a stupid question and don't let others control your perceptions. Judge for yourself.

Stephen Harper prides himself on the image he presents. It is up to Canadians to look beyond the clothes and judge the inner man.

END NOTES

1. *Ed. Note*: Leo Strauss (1899-1973) was a political philosopher whose Machiavellian doctrines, many contemporary intellectuals argue, helped shape neo-conservative ideology and has in particular influenced the architects of current U.S. foreign and domestic policies. In essence, Strauss defends the political pragmatism of, among others, Machiavelli, Nietzsche and Plato, whose concept of the 'noble lie' forms Strauss' own conception that there is virtue in the political art of secrecy and lies to help the wise retain control over the vulgar. The elite (or the wise) must obscure their objectives to protect them from reprisal of the common people (the vulgar), who are not wise enough to know what is good for them. For more on the complexity of Straussian philosophy, recommended reading includes: *The Political Ideas of Leo Strauss* by Shadia B. Drury (New York: St. Martin's Press, 1988); *Leo Strauss: An Introduction to His Thoughts and Intellectual Legacy* by Thomas L. Pangle (Baltimore: The John Hopkins University Press, 2006); *Leo Strauss and the Politics of American Empire* by Anne Norton (New Haven & London: Yale University Press, 2004); and Strauss' own *Thoughts on Machiavelli* (Glencoe, Ill: The Free Press, 1958).

2. "Day, Holland clash over Zaccardelli allegation." CBC.ca. 8 December 2006. <http://www.cbc.ca/canada/story/2006/12/07/arar-day.html>

3. Gray, Tony. *The Story of Alfred Nobel, the Peace Prize and the Laureate: Champions of Peace.* United Kingdom: Paddington Press Ltd, 1976, pg. 239.

New Clothes

Once, not too far away nor long before,
A new king ruled from shore to shore to shore.
A proud man, he vowed to transform the land,
He'd rule his kingdom with an iron hand.

The king was wise, ordered fine new attire,
These rich threads would mask his inner desire.
Advisors found clothes that met his request,
Brought them quickly forth at the king's behest.

The king was aghast, they showed him thin air,
With these new clothes he'd be totally bare.
"Just try them on once and you'll understand,
Peasants will find you most regally grand."

The king trusted their words, put on the gown,
Strolled through the market of a nearby town.
Sure enough, people cheered in sheer delight,
The king presented a most stylish sight.

The king was thrilled, barely contained his joy,
His subjects were sheep, wouldn't notice this ploy.
"Now I'll live my dream and my new disguise,
Will shield my deep desire from everyone's eyes."

And true to his word, he plotted and planned,
"The world will marvel at my great new land!"
He set his sights on all that was cherished,
What he wished for he would soon accomplish.

CHAPTER ONE

A CANADA YOU WON'T RECOGNIZE

A country depends on the heart of men;
it is miniscule if the heart is small,
and immense if the heart is great.
                    Simone Schwartz-Bart

Canadians are the people who learned
to live without the bold accents of
the natural ego-trippers of other lands.
                    Marshall McLuhan

After the Conservative victory on January 23rd, 2006, many Canadians fretted over the future of their Canada and were concerned that the new Prime Minister, Stephen Harper, would take the country in an unfamiliar and unwanted neo-conservative direction, more in line with U.S. Republicans than with Canadian tradition.

The Conservatives now held 125 seats, the Liberals 102, and the NDP 29, with one independent. It will be interesting to observe how Harper views minority governance. Will he be aggressive in implementing his image of Canada or will he be cooperative? Some predict that he will follow the latter approach until such time that he can form a majority government, enabling him to implement radical changes unacceptable to most Canadians.

Time will tell.

A Prayer for Canada

Now I lay me down to weep,
pray, the Lord, our environment keep
from he who cares less than one iota,
and aims to scrap the accord Kyoto.

Please ask him, Lord, to lower his sights,
and withhold his attack on human rights.
Please don't diminish our southern frontier,
his friend, George Bush, is already too near.

To our dear children, please be more fair,
and reconsider our precious day-care.
Keep federalism strong, we as one,
Canada sans Québec would be no fun.

Please never let church mix with state,
this would be a most horrible fate.
For all who want to remain free,
Guard the principles of democracy.

Blessed are our poor, save them from strife,
the sick and the homeless, defend with your life.
Please let him understand and always care,
Life for some has never been fair.

Value the oppressed, preserve all their rights,
take charity and hope into new great heights.
Promote world peace and our reputation,
as a trustworthy and honest mediating nation.

We ask you, dear Lord, if you truly care,
don't let him devastate our Medicare.
I pray, my dear Lord, with all of my might,
please save us all from the very Far Right.

Amen

Prime Minister Harper, International Trade Minister David Emerson and Canada's ambassador to the U.S. Michael Wilson cut a deal that ended the longstanding softwood lumber dispute with the United States. Critics across Canada called it a sell-out, the end of free trade and freewheeling politicking. The Prime Minister conceded in excess of one billion dollars of illegally collected U.S. tariffs (as determined by NAFTA panels) to expedite the agreement. It was anticipated that a large percentage of this money would go to the war chests of American lumber companies to offset their litigation costs against Canada that had accumulated during the dispute. Free trade became regulated trade with quotas and mechanisms that would initiate new taxes. And David Emerson, former C.E.O. of Canfor Corporation, Canada's largest lumber exporter, needed vindication for crossing the floor. Harper also hoped that the electorate would view the new PM as a man of action. In contrast, many simply looked upon him as a political opportunist. Harper relinquished hard-earned legal ground for a flawed solution that simply demonstrated that he had not met one pre-election promise.

David Wilkins, the U.S. Ambassador to Canada, certainly had his concerns allayed that Canada's relationship with her southern neighbor was on "a slippery slope," as he had suggested to the then-Prime Minister Martin during the election campaign.[1]

Speaking of sell-outs, Harper's corner man in his election campaign, former Prime Minister Brian Mulroney, had previously conceded Canada's control over our own oil resources to the States as part of the Free Trade Agreement, a concession that still exists today. Clayton Yeutter, the U.S. chief trade negotiator for the deal, commented on October 3, 1987, "We've signed a stunning new trade pact with Canada. The Canadians don't know what they have signed. In twenty years, they will be sucked into the US economy."[2] Mulroney's legacy is alive and well, thriving in the backroom decision-making of Canada's "new' government.

Beutel 2007   beutoons @ yahoo.com

Billion Dollar Baby

"So, ya wanta fight, boy," the old man spat.
"Ya gotta get rid of some of that fat,
you need to do some serious trainin', kid,
then we'll be lookin' at a championship bid."

Mulroney shook his head, "You're kinda pink.
We'll go pretty far," he said with a wink.
"First I'll put together just the right bunch,
then I'll show you how to throw a mean punch."

His eyes grew misty, his nostalgia soared,
of bygone wins, like the Free Trade Accord.
"So I lost our oil control, it's no big deal!"
The Yankees had laughed, the pact was a steal.

Training camp was tough, a grueling affair,
news was scarce, for the press was banned there.
Stephen skipped rope, soon he learned how to spar,
Emerged then one day as the new "hard-assed" star.

At last it arrived, the championship day,
Stevie J. was pumped, his spirit was gay.
He slid down the ramp, his caucus in tow,
cheering and yelping, they made quite the show.

Sporting star-spangled trunks, he flexed his might,
with Brian on his left, Wilkins on his right.
They cursed through their lips, "Damn media blight,
how dare they attend this sovereignty fight!"

Harper's opponent, in maple leaf gear,
stood utterly alone, bristling with fear.
Referee Wilson, a pro with these fights,
coolly delivered Canada's last rites.

The crowd cheered wildly, an exciting night,
Emerson took bets with peripheral sight.
Following his instincts oft saved the day,
he well remembered Vancouver-Kingsway.

Steve's fight was flawless, he shuffled with glee,
flew like a butterfly, stung like a bee.
The western Rocky struck with cunning stealth,
Rice pranced on canvas, announcing the twelfth.

The scrap soon ended that trans-border war,
Bush, McKay and Flaherty all marked their score.
With Wilson's tally, there was no maybe,
Steve was crowned the Billion Dollar Baby.

Canada's First Nation peoples' early fears about the Conservatives forming the new government became a reality. Many native leaders had great misgivings about Tom Flanagan leading Harper's election campaign, and then becoming a senior adviser to the new Prime Minister. Native people had criticized Mr. Flanagan, a former professor at the University of Calgary (Stephen Harper's Alma Mater), for his views on land claims, reserves and native assimilation. Since coming to power, Harper has belittled and dismissed the Kelowna Accord, a historic agreement hammered out over 18 months and agreed to by Aboriginals, all provinces and territories, and the Liberal government. With a $5.1 billion allocation over five years, it would have improved shameful deficiencies in education, housing and infrastructure in native communities. In comparison, the Conservative budget offered a mere $150 million in 2006 and $300 million in 2007.

During a CPAC interview with Indian Affairs Minister Jim Prentice in the Commons Foyer, New Democrat MP Charlie Angus and Chief Leo Friday of the Kashechewan Nation approached to ask the Minister if his party would honour the previous government's agreement to relocate the community and build new houses to counteract the recurring flooding problem and consequent health problems. Mr. Prentice abruptly turned his back on the chief and walked away without speaking. In Question Period, Mr. Prentice had spoken about the need for consultation with Aboriginals prior to taking any action.[3]

Meanwhile, Tory MP Brian Fitzpatrick had recently suggested that Aboriginals live in a "Marxist paradise." As a member of the Canadian Alliance Party, he had once joked about being "scalped" at an all-candidates meeting.[4] Public outrage quickly resulted in his apology.

The Conservatives frivolously, yet strategically, had scattered seed money to entice the Canadian electorate to give the party a majority in the next election. Thanks to Paul Martin and his Liberals, Harper's government had inherited very robust coffers, yet they couldn't find the funds to improve Aboriginal living conditions.

As Long as the Green Grass Shall Grow
(Broken Promises, Broken Treaties)

As long as the green grass shall grow,
as long as the clear rivers shall flow,
all our people shall be safe and warm,
our spirits shall save us from harm.

We praise the keepers of our lands,
shielding her bounty with strong hands.
Our ancestors shall protect our ground,
the harvest of nature shall abound.

Colonel Harper coldly rides against our sleeping village,
bluecoats striking heartlessly in despicable pillage.
General Flanagan observes from his place on the knoll,
as they add more weakened Aboriginals to their toll.

From smallpox to tuberculosis, will our plight never end?
The elitists are merciless, our spirits they offend.
Our housing is moldy, our clean water is long gone,
Lieutenant Prentice ran from the chief of Kashechewan.

Sergeant Fitzpatrick, a rising man from C-Patrol,
circled metaphoric wagons, then trying to be droll,
Suggested our people live in a Marxist paradise,
had lost fear of being "scalped" and any other demise.

Broken treaties have long clouded our unfortunate past.
How long can these degrading social injustices last?
The death of Kelowna, a most telling indication,
of Canada's leaders and their care for the First Nation.

First they abandon our children then abandon our lands,
to the perils of climate change while shielding the Tar Sands.
The treaty Kyoto the PM flippantly derailed,
as protector of Nature, he has appallingly failed.

As long as the green grass shall grow,
and as long as the springs still flow,
our spirits shall remain forever strong,
to right this unspeakable wrong.

July 1, 2006. A joyful day on Parliament Hill as people gathered to commemorate Canada Day. It was also a time to reflect upon our past, our present and our future direction as a nation, both at home and abroad.

Happy Birthday Canada!

One hundred thirty-nine candles dancing in a red blaze,
while Canadians rejoice in diverse lighthearted ways.
A time for reflection, to consider who we are,
judging by our fate and those living afar.

The host grins widely, shakes hands, calls all the shots,
skillfully works the crowd, shrewdly seeks the best photo ops.
A decorated veteran, a sweet minority child.
Oh, a baby in arms, all the mothers will go wild!

His blue-suited bodyguards, ensuring nothing is amiss,
watch out for terrorists, or worse, insurgent journalists.
An uncontrolled variable which cannot be programmed,
to bolster his public image. Oh well, the press be damned!

How can we judge our country with our PM at the wheel?
Hard to cut through rhetoric and get at what is real.
Think about his declaration of the Five-Point Plan,
quickly hid the important, it reeks of old-fashioned flimflam.

Take a moment and consider the unspoken intent,
what appears as the agenda of this smooth talking gent.
The first we can consider to be most alarming,
the world cringed in horror as he dismissed global warming.

Kyoto, Smyoto, he soundly kicked it in the touche,
forsook world leadership, kowtowed to George Bush.
He called for voluntary measures, oh wouldn't that be nice,
except for the telltale melting of our far northern ice.

Scrap climate change research and cut EnerGuide,
their razor-sharp axes flew while the environment fried.
Respond to Suzuki and all others who have tried,
let science and the globe's peril guide his dark ages pride.

Then the Kelowna Accord, yet another big bust,
the wounded Aboriginals left writhing in his dust.
Joined Russia at the UN, once more kept them in his sights,
and voted against recognition of indigenous rights.

Our soldiers' repatriation, also tainted by his hand,
set off a cry from their parents and most in our land.
Caught in an unflattering light, he shuffled then he ran,
placing the blame on the head of an aging army man.

Also cached in his agenda, the wooing of Quebec,
but even this vote mongering is becoming a wreck.
UNESCO, Afghanistan, Kyoto, federal dole,
no industry or worker protection, *ce n'est pas drôle!*

Signed the sellout softwood deal, doing all his own way,
to his friend George W. Bush, he wished a Happy Birthday!
Ignored cries of industry, seized a flawed solution
that killed NAFTA's Chapter 19 dispute resolution.

Like a crazed moth to light, attracted to Bush's mentor lure,
he committed the Armed Forces at the cost of Darfur.
Peacekeeping is a heartfelt Canadian tradition,
not Enduring Freedom with its seek-and-destroy mission.

The Canada childcare programme he scrapped in a heartbeat,
A head start for our youngest, no advantage for the elite.
Assailed our children's future, our country's upcoming hope,
without affordable care, their families cannot possibly cope.

The party is over and the guests wind their way down the Hill
by the eternal flame, they pause to toss a coin, quite hopeful still
that our country stays distinct and safeguards our reputation,
as people who care for others as a peace-loving nation.

In what appears to have been a feeble attempt to distance the Prime Minister from American foreign policy, Foreign Affairs Minister Peter MacKay hosted U.S. Secretary of State Condoleeza Rice in his home riding in Nova Scotia, far from the nation's capital. Rice spoke briefly about Canada's generosity to American air travelers during the 9/11 aftermath. More tellingly, she extolled and profusely thanked Canada on behalf of the U.S. for its military involvement in Afghanistan, thereby emphasizing her boss' strong desire for Canada to stay the course and remain in sync with his global war on terrorism.

Rumours flew as a result of the very cordial visit between the host and his guest. The truth of the matter, however, lies in the very cozy relationship that has developed between Harper and Bush.

The Dream Team

Matchmaker, matchmaker, won't you please make me a match,
Wouldn't Foreign Minister Peter make a nice yummy catch?
Romance in the morning sipping a double-double,
connecting with you will be so very little trouble.
You know I kept the window wide, and I heard the ocean,
our cross-border romance has Bushed into motion.

Our countries are now bedfellows, we dance cheek to cheek,
with all of your nice resources, there's no chance we'll be weak.
Our foreign policies are indistinguishable,
let's rendezvous at Tim Hortons in Kabul?
No, you say? In Kandahar? You are my spring tonic.
How could she have dumped you, that Liberal turncoat Stronach!

On the Hill, Stephen organized a preacher's event,
Condemned those who dared question, fall on your knees and repent.
Flanked by soldiers, their loved ones, twin tower families,
what a timely opportunity he'd chosen to seize.
Read out his decree with an egotistical twist,
Prepare now to "… accept enormous sacrifice and risk!"

With Bush-like guile, Stephen played his fear-mongering hand,
fight or flight instincts would surely recapture his land.
Bully all dissenters, charge each one with non-support,
Dialogue and free expression he'd always try and abort.
Many more now are cautious of his controlling way.
let's hope freedom's principles will once more rule the day.

Stephen Harper's leadership style is worthy of close scrutiny. It involves a somewhat instinctive approach that shrewdly reads each new situation and responds in a manner that will optimize survival in the public eye.

One strategy is to strike to achieve a questionable objective, then quickly counterbalance it with the diversion of the public to an unrelated, seemingly altruistic action. The classic example is Harper's cancellation of the national childcare programme that would have improved the lives of countless Canadians through the development of new childcare spaces. To counter this negative, he announced that it was every family's right to choose how their children were cared for, and then sugared his commitment to "democratic choice" with a monthly cheque of one hundred dollars. It may appear good in theory, but it's very devastating in the long term.

Another favorite strategy is bullying. If forest industries didn't accept the softwood deal, the government threatened that it would no longer provide its support to fight the U.S. lawyers. Yet another example of Harpo-bullying: If you don't support Senate reform, you are the enemy of democracy.

Seed doubt when necessary. Yes, some scientists are concerned about climate change, but the final word isn't in on whether or not human activity is causing it. Therefore, don't get carried away with Kyoto. We'll eventually do something about greenhouse gases.

When accused of a bad deed, quickly point your finger at someone else: Don't reprimand *me* … Look at what *they* did!

After canceling worthwhile and proven social programmes, say it was necessary to "trim the fat" to ensure that taxpayers' dollars were not being squandered. And, by the way, that extra money that we saved? It'll go back into your pockets … Beats worrying about others!

And finally, control the message and continually tell Canadians about the wonderful job we are doing. What do you mean we aren't doing things right? Haven't you been listening to us?

Stephen Harper is definitely the Maestro of the House.

Maestro of the House

Maestro of the House
Stepping on the press
Setting up a photo op
Deflecting voters' stress
Spins a sticky web
Throws the crowd a scrap
Steps on the vulnerable
And doesn't give a crap

Pidgin-holing his enemies
Throws around his weight
Calling them unpatriotic
Then denying true debate
Everyone loves a winner
Ask him and he'll agree
Doing whatsoever he pleases
And t'hell with democracy

Maestro of the House
Shepherd of the range
Hides behind the smog
Denying climate change
Spins a sticky web
Throws the crowd a crumb
Plays on your emotions
Thinking folks are dumb

Avoiding all the questions
Spins reality
Hey all the Liberals
Are anti-Israeli
Everyone loves a doer
Who gets the job done fast
He's selling out O Canada
As her people groan and gasp

Maestro of the House
Keeps his crowds in line
They won't raise an eyebrow
To a man divine
Spins a sticky web
Throws the crowd some bread
Tramples the illiterate
Their fault to be unread

Blaming the ones before him
When something goes amuck
Why should he be forthright
Just simply pass the buck
Everyone loves a smoothy
So please stop your bitchin'
To hell with Status of Women
Just put 'em in the kitchen

Maestro of the House
Ruler of the press
Ignore those who question
The public couldn't care less
Spins a sticky web
Gives the rich a tweak
The fate of those in need
Has never been so bleak

Smiling his way through governance
Control's his *soupe du jour*
Economics guide his hand
Pas les sentiments du coeur
Everyone loves a Maestro
Ask him and you will see
Why should I compromise
It's me and me and me

Maestro of the House
Keeper of the blues
A billion to the Yanks
Now watch ya got to lose
Spins a sticky web
Throws the crowd a noose
Better do it my way
Or I will cook your goose

Playing with his suit coat
Purring at his quips
When push comes down to shove
He doesn't give a whit
Everyone loves a winner
Ask him and you will see
This neo-con wins the prize for
Egocentricity.

The people of Kashechewan, a small Cree community on Ontario's James Bay coast, have endured extreme hardship, from tainted drinking water to squalid living conditions caused by flooding of their houses and exacerbated by subsequent emergency evacuations. In October of 2005, the government of the day had developed a plan to build fifty new houses each year for the next decade on higher ground near the Albany River, just upstream from the current location. Upon their election, the Conservative government promptly buried the hatchet into this proposal. Indian Affairs Minister Jim Prentice then engaged Alan Pope, a former Ontario Tory MP, to study alternatives for the Kashechewan community. He came up with five possibilities that included the Liberals' previous proposal to relocate upstream, although even if this option were to be ultimately accepted, it would certainly involve a lengthy study and a substantial delay. He strongly recommended relocation to the outskirts of Timmins - a mere air flight away from their traditional land!

Interestingly to note, DeBeers plans to open Ontario's first diamond mine near Kashechewan in 2008. Would the people's absence affect the Cree's claim to the land surrounding this natural resource? Wouldn't new job opportunities solve the unemployment and social problems that currently exist and create a very positive and healthy environment? Unfortunately, a desperate situation leads to desperate measures and the people will naturally be tempted and subtly pressured to accept the government's proposal. There is also the real danger of setting a precedent with other Aboriginal lands.

In light of the Tory's cancellation of the Kelowna Accord, which would have allocated over $5 billion for a badly needed improvement of Aboriginal life in Canada, one speculates that the government is promoting the assimilation of Canada's First People into non-Aboriginal society. Their treatment has been appalling.

Rod Bruinooge, Conservative MP and Secretary to the Indian Affairs Minister, launched a disgustingly personal and partisan attack against Paul Martin during the former Prime Minister's appearance before the Aboriginal Affairs Committee.[5] Bruinooge ridiculed Martin's defense of the Kelowna Accord and labeled it worthless because it was unsigned, although Canada's Aboriginal groups and all of the provinces and territories had publicly agreed to this landmark agreement.

Colonel Harper's Revenge

There are strange things done in Kashechewan
By white men who slither in oil,
Great resources abound in the far north,
Where diamonds and gold are soil.

A luxury to leave these lands so untouched,
If a super power we'll ever be,
Burn the treaties, then assimilate all,
They'll quickly be absorbed, you'll see.

Agent Prentice sent word out from Ottawa,
with words both flowery and sweet.
We want the best for our good native friends,
Who I'll always be ready to meet.

Later while walking outside the Commons,
The Kashechewan chief came near,
But Agent Prentice rode off in a gallop,
In a cloud of fury and fear.

But our water is bad, our houses are moldy,
Our lives have gone from bad to worse.
Help us in our time of need and despair,
Help save our dignity from this curse.

Our traditional ways are being jeopardized,
Our culture again laid to waste,
We're still hurting from our ghosts residential,
We're in prison because of our race.

With ease, schemes emerged from the War Office,
An emissary they had sent there.
He delivered a papal-like pronouncement,
That seemed to be totally fair.

We present to you five varied options,
The choice will remain in your hands,
We suggest you follow the one that leads
You far from your ancestral lands.

They had learned a good trick from their history,
Starving out Chief Sitting Bull's tribe.
If a people are suffering badly,
They'll surely give into a bribe.

Your spirit may demand the Albany,
We turfed this idea before.
We'll do a feasibility study.
Do you mind suffering some more?

Meanwhile, back at the War Office...

Bruinooge sat cross-legged before the fire,
His poison-tipped tongue spat out grief.
Heed these words, never again shall you speak,
I'm the envoy of the White Chief.

What is this about that Kelowna Accord?
Do honour to the White Man's word?
So you all smoked in complete agreement!
This unsigned treaty is absurd!

You're a toothless white chief and you reek of lies,
When you voice all your paltry fears.
I'm a brave voice of this new land of ours.
The First Nation will pay with their tears.

The energy moguls looked on with hope,
That a precedent would soon be set,
Prospectors drooled in salacious delight,
As the Bluecoats tossed out their net.

G reat shades of Dicken's 19th century England!

In a time of affluence and an extraordinary $13 billion pay down of the national debt, the Conservative government made harsh cuts that affected the most marginalized people of Canada. Fulfilling a campaign promise to cut $1 billion of spending, they indiscriminately slashed programmes and services that bit hard at the social fabric of this country.

Jim Flaherty, former financial hit man of Mike Harris' Common Sense Revolution, radically cut funds safeguarding language and equality rights as well as reducing support for women's shelters, literacy programmes, non-profit organizations, museums, and youth employment programmes to name a few.

Chop! The Court Challenges Programme, which gave citizens without the financial wherewithal the ability to challenge court decisions on Charter and Constitutional rights, noisily fell. The Prime Minister could not fathom the provision of money that would be used to fight the government. An obvious spin-off of the neo-conservative belief that those in power always know best and are very unlikely to make mistakes that affect rights!

Chop! The government closed twelve of sixteen Status of Women offices. Non-governmental groups could no longer access federal funds for women's advocacy. You've come a long way baby, but maybe you've come far enough!

The Tories made these cuts arbitrarily without the appropriate consultative process. The Dickensian tragedy of poverty and orphanages stimulates reflection on their cancellation of the National Child Care Programme. Their broken election promise to not touch Income Trust resulted in not only lost confidence in the government's word, but also the loss of millions of dollars of pension security for the elderly.

An excerpt from
Stefagin with a Twist

(Stefagin)
In my life, coin is big,
Huge full bags, gold I dig!
I fear it doesn't come easy,
You've got to slash a programme or two.

It doesn't come easy, boys,
You've got to slash a programme or two.

(Backroom Boys)
Fear it isn't breezy,
You've got to slash a programme or two!

(Stefagin)
Let's show Jim what to do. What say you, my backroom boys?

(Backroom Boys)
Tell him the way it is, boss!

(Stefagin)
Who needs a "welfare state"?

In the cold, chose their mess,
Cut our taxes, give the buggers less!
The homeless aren't our worry, Jim,
You've got to slash a programme or two.

Throw the homeless in jail, Jim,
You've got to slash a programme or two!

(Backroom Boys)
Stuff it in their ear, Jim,
You've got to slash a programme or two!

(Stefagin)
Let's not forget the pretty ladies…

Women's rights, what a crock!
Put 'em in the kitchen, in a frock!
Advocacy's a waste of our time, Jim,
You've got to slash a programme or two.

Got to got to keep them busy in the kitchen, Jim,
You've got to slash a programme or two!

(Backroom Boys)
Barefoot and pregnant in the kitchen, Jim,
You've got to slash a programme or two!

(Stefagin)
And what about those snotty-nosed children?

Bratty kids, out of sight,
No care spaces? Serves you right!
They just have to keep them at home, Jim,
You've got to slash a programme or two.

Need to stash them away at home, Jim,
You've got to slash a programme or two!

(Backroom Boys)
Out of sight and out of mind, Jim,
You've got to slash a programme or two!

(Stefagin)
What d'ya mean ya can't read?

Here's a book, take a look,
Don't get the words? What a smook!
Now they can eat their words, Jim,
You've got to slash a programme or two.

Lost their chance, can eat their words,
You've got to slash a programme or two!

(Backroom Boys)
Blew their chance, can eat their words,
You've got to slash a programme or two!

(Stefagin)
Imagine that, worried about their rights!

Feel oppressed, what a shame!
So you're poor, your claim to fame.
Feed them money to defy us, Jim?
You've got to slash a programme or two.

Let them fight their own battles, Jim,
You've got to slash a programme or two!

(Backroom Boys)
Absurd to help them sue us, Jim,
You've got to slash a programme or two!

(Stefagin)
Look at that smug old goat!

White haired man, toddling past,
Trying to make his pension last.
Hit him when he's not looking, Jim,
You've got to slash a programme or two.

Much too secure, ought to be poor,
You've got to slash a programme or two!

(Backroom Boys)
All too secure, hard to endure,
You've got to slash a programme or two!

(Stefagin)
Get out there and fix it, Jim!

Help the poor, help the distressed,
Shelling out money, I get depressed.
There's only one thing that helps me through,
I've got to slash a programme or two,
Wouldn't you?
Got to slash a programme or two!

Prime Minister Harper honoured his campaign promise to reintroduce the same-sex marriage issue in Parliament, although MPs had already passed a law in 2005 legalizing these unions. His action smacked of the ingenuous in that he would have to call on the Constitution's notwithstanding clause to override the Charter on this issue that would cause quite a stir on the democratic front. Harper had previously stated that this would not happen.

His decision would satisfy the wishes of the far right traditionalists; however, it would also alienate those who wanted the issue buried. Many felt that the reopening of the file would create unnecessary divisiveness throughout the country and would once again negatively centre out a minority group.

The carefully worded motion read as follows: "to introduce legislation to restore the traditional definition of marriage without affecting civil unions and while respecting existing same-sex marriages."[6] This wording neatly avoided the pitfall of actually introducing legislation that could immediately bring a change in the definition, were it to be accepted. An interesting tactic!

The Prime Minister, known for his knack of turning questionable circumstances into supposedly win-win situations, gave his MPs a free vote. To win the vote would create negative feelings towards the Tories by the majority of the electorate. To not reopen the issue would create fallout with his traditionalist power base.

MPs voted 175 to 123 against the motion. The Prime Minister voted in its favor while several of his high-powered Cabinet Ministers voted against it. This could be construed as a very shrewd move. Harper's personal vote would maintain the confidence of his base group while the dissension of key Conservative MPs would placate the majority of Canadians who thought the whole process was a waste of time.

Moreover, allowing a free vote would suggest to people that Harper was not as controlling as many people had thought, although some wondered if his actions were a more subtle and disguised form of control that would lead to the desired end result in the long run.

"We made a promise to have a free vote on this issue... and obviously the vote was decisive."[7] With his words, the Prime Minister had covered all bases. He indicated that he did not foresee reopening this question in the future. All the strings tied off, the present had been neatly wrapped and prominently positioned under the tree for Christmas!

Charter Hiccup

The blue ribbon won, an action deemed bold,
The "new" P.M. proudly brought home the gold.
Undaunted by the win of past court fights,
He took aim at gay and lesbian rights.

Quite the quandary, it seemed so at first,
But oft you salvage the best from the worst.
He weighed the options, chose a win-win path,
Mapped his journey with an arrogant laugh.

An election vow he chose to address.
Revisited same sex marriage, took bad press,
Appeased the base of traditional views,
Then called for a vote he wanted to lose.

Stephen, advised by a personal guru,
Took his sound advice about what to do.
In a chamber viewed his magic mirror,
That always said what he wanted to hear.

They mused on upheaving personal rights,
His House motion raised him to nasty heights!
A loud knock, a voice cried in frantic woe,
"Can ya please hurry up, I gotta go!"

Opposition decried his roguish play,
Charter advocates watched in full dismay.
"Enough is enough, don't split our country!
Just lead us all to peace and harmony!"

A "wild" debate raged, but just for one day,
So stirring, most chose to stay far away!
The arguments were so profoundly deep,
Surprising to say, they didn't fall asleep!

Bruinooge gave his views on the colour wheel,
Yellow plus red makes orange, the real deal!
Marriage is just like mixing on canvas,
Two of the same? Well, you might just as well pass!

Harper thought, gave his caucus a "free vote,"
Shed his control image, perchance his hope?
Ministers cried out their nay decision,
Saved the Tories from public derision!

Stephen was placed in the Hill's Hall of Fame,
Threatened freedom for convenient gain.
Not done by a leader since World War II,
Marginalized others, this callous Blue!

Human rights, the stuff of democracy,
Image underscored by fragility.
Small steps lead to a free nation's demise,
Beware of a wolf in a sheep's disguise.

P rime Minister Harper has taken on a formidable force - Canada's women. About four hundred staged a protest on Parliament Hill. Heritage Minister Bev Oda had announced a funding cut of $5 million to the Status of Women Canada.

This organization is a federally sponsored government agency that encourages the participation of women in social, political, cultural and economic life in Canada. One very important function was to provide grants to lobby groups. To add insult to the injury of the cuts, women's groups that wished to advocate, lobby or research in the realm of rights were no longer eligible for funding.

This was no surprise in that the Prime Minister had previously cut the Court Challenges Programme. His philosophy is why give people the financial wherewithal to fight the government? He apparently has a notion that those in power (at least the Conservatives) are beyond reproach.

Minister Oda stated that the money saved could better be used to help women with their daily problems in their own communities. If this was truly Harper's only concern, the Tories could have pulled the needed funds from their large surplus to maintain the advocacy element. In addition, critics believe that this re-channeling of money would pit local organizations against the national groups that are better able to deal with the larger picture and can affect change on a countrywide basis.

Joanne Hussey, along with four other Halifax women, started a campaign against Harper's cuts. She maintained that the Prime Minister owed her twenty-nine cents, which is the disparity between the sexes on every dollar earned.

Their web site is http://www.thewomenareangry.org.

The Gender Bender
(Father Knows Best)

The rally cry sounded, they climbed through the noon mist,
their blood raged hot as they sought the chauvinist.
Battle scarred women guardedly mounted the Hill,
loathe to swallow the PM's poison pill.

We seek justice, return the word equality,
pass laws that secure our pay equity.
Save advocacy for the Status of Women,
to be treated the same is not sinning.

Please restore funding, why treat us with such distaste
Respect our gender, our worth don't lay waste.
Restore the Challenge Programme, safeguard our frail rights,
Our status grew from painful hard-won fights.

Harper dispatched foot soldier Bev to make cuts,
slashed with her sword, their programmes to gut.
A heartless axe-man, chopped millions from their chest,
In her mind believed that Stephen knew best.

Private Hussey cried out, this defies common sense,
for each buck, Harper owes twenty-nine cents.
We've been reduced to simple participation,
Second class citizens - Shame on the nation!

Sergeant Oda courageously faced all the heat,
Father Steve tittered, content with his feat.
It worked out flawlessly as he had surmised,
one pen stroke left women disenfranchised.

During the 2006 election campaign, Stephen Harper promised a $1 billion cut in government spending. Under the careful guidance of his leader, Harper's Finance Minister Jim Flaherty directed, without appropriate consultation, the elimination of programmes that hurt the needy and reduced funding in areas that helped make Canada an envied country. Harper kept his promise, but at great cost to Canadian people. He affected mean-spirited cuts in spite of inheriting a $13 billion government surplus. Furthermore, his broken promise to not touch Income Trusts resulted in a shattering hit on many pensioners and those planning for a secure retirement.

Adding fuel to the fire, Harper continued to give oil and gas companies in Canada an annual billion-dollar tax break, money that could have been used to maintain the status quo in government spending or used to decrease the companies' greenhouse gas production. They are the source of the increased emissions that have made it difficult to meet our legally binding Kyoto targets.

Minister Flaherty introduced a plan to eliminate our country's "net debt" by the year 2021. This is a smokescreen meant to create the illusion that the Conservatives are doing an exceptional job in the finance field. The notion is entirely misleading.

To calculate the net debt, all federal and provincial government debts are added together, and then assets like the Canada and Québec Pension Plans are used in a calculation to reduce the debt. These assets belong to Canadians alone and not the government. How gullible do they think Canadians are? Forget the use of this archaic term "net debt," and stick with what Canadians are familiar with – national debt.

Tory Top Gun

Lock your doors and windows, a new gun's on the street,
A slinger with a fast draw, a man hard to beat.
His name's James, not of Brothers' notoriety,
A dead-eye shot from the famed Mike Harris Party.

His repute stretched afar, Bytown learned of his speed,
Sagebrush Steve knew this hombre could fill a big need.
Things needed to be done, he sent an urgent wire,
Knew James reacted fast when he came under fire.

They bonded mighty fast, chaps cut from the same stuff,
Blood brothers to the end when the going got tough.
James took to his job like a bee takes to honey,
A fierce hired gun when it came down to money.

James cleaned up that town, just like lickitty split,
Wasn't too hard to take money from the unfit.
Grabbed a billion in bullion, slid it to Sagebrush,
Who staked his prospectors in the western oil rush.

Bytown thrived, swiftly disposed of its net debt,
Sagebrush earmarked their savings, took all he could get.
This saga to all generations shall be told,
To get what you desire, you need simply be bold.

ENDNOTES

1."Martin rejects US Ambassador's rebuke." CBC.ca. 13 December 2005. <http://www.cbc.ca/news/story/2005/12/13/wilkins-051213.html>

2."Timeline of the Progress toward a North American Union." ViveleCanada. ca. 19 September 2006. <http://www.vivelecanada.ca/staticpages/index. php/20060830133702539>

3."Tory MP in hot seat over Aboriginal Paradise remarks." Canada.com. 02 June 2006. <"http://www.canada.com/topics/news/politics/story. html?id=ffa62480-f5b5-47f3-becd- 9ce5033ed37e&k=41211>

4.39th Parliament, 1st Session, Standing Committee on Aboriginal Affairs and Northern Development. Number 025, 09 November 2006. <http://209.85.165.104/search?q=cache:LGdU3pys44YJ:cmte.parl.gc.ca/ Content/HOC/Committee/391/AANO/Evidence/EV2499050/AANO-EV25->

5."Parliament Debates Restoring Traditional Marriage." CTV.ca. 07 December 2006. <http://www.ctv.ca/servlet/ArticleNews/story/CTVNews/20061205/ dion_ssm_061206/ 20061206?hub=TopStories>

6."PM declares same-sex issue closed." Canoe.ca. 08 December 2006. <http://cnews.canoe.ca/CNEWS/Canada/2006/12/05/2638191-cp.html>

CHAPTER TWO

🇨🇦

LIFE IS MY HIGHWAY

*Sometimes I wonder whether the world is being run by
smart people who are putting us on
or by imbeciles who really mean it.*
Mark Twain

*When a man is wrapped up in himself
he makes a pretty small package.*
John Ruskin

Prime Minister Harper and his International Trade Minister, David Emerson, announced the resolution of the long-standing softwood lumber dispute between Canada and the United States. Deemed a sell-out by many in the lumber industry, Conservatives were nonetheless ecstatic that they had quickly ended the dispute and were extremely self-complementary in spite of Canada-wide criticism.

In summation, Mr. Emerson stated that the Harper government was focused and not easily distracted by "the little things." Mr. Emerson added that "... in the past, there was always a kind of a soft, mushy exercise with, like a waterbed, you press here, and it pops up somewhere else." He further asserted that Mr. Harper is "...unambiguous, he's committed, and willing to be very firm and resolved..."[1] As well, Mr. Emerson had just recently created a flurry in the media when he described his boss as being "hard-assed."

Soft and Mushy

Strange bedfellows are part of political fare,
on a soft and mushy bed.
You deftly press here, it pops up rigidly there,
it's ever so easy to get ahead.

We won't be distracted by "all those little things,"
notre ménage à countless.
Like behind-the-scene deals and our sleazy flings,
often referred to by the damn press.

David praised Steve for being firm and committed,
he was always a close pillow friend.
There'll be no more softwood dispute, then admitted,
we'll be "hard-assed" right to the end.

Stephen Harper attended a trilateral summit in Cancún, Mexico with his NAFTA partners, Presidents Bush and Fox. At the end of the summit, the "three amigos," as the media dubbed them, made summary statements about their meetings. Prime Minister Harper elected to deliver the majority of his speech in French, making one wonder why, when coming from a bilingual country, he continued to emphasize one language over the other. Harper should not tamper with the strong mutual respect that already exists between the two language groups in his obvious attempt to gain more acceptances in Québec.

Viva Cancún!

In Cancún Steve planned to put together his name,
Hoping to fix his lagging-at-home fame.
He thought, how can I spin it?
I know I can win it.
It just calls for a politicking game.

After winning seats from the Parti Québecois,
Hoped to be crowned Québec's newest "roi-roi!"
But come the next election,
Saw more Bloc defection.
"Je vais y gagner encore une fois!"

He giggled then thought, "Oh, what the heck!
I'll do this for you, my *cher Québec!*"
Spoke all almost in French,
Anglos on the backbench.
His bad choices we've learn to expect.

Singing Our Home and Our Native Land,
"I'll rule my realm with an iron hand.
I'll dazzle you with moves,
With my wits, I'll never lose.
I'm the Stevie Harper One-Man-Band!"

Although many Canadians may have initially been impressed by the Conservatives' budget, closer inspection revealed a deliberate, focused seeding of limited tax credits and payouts to potential voters, a slashing of most environmental programmes, and very notably, an about-face on the needs of Canada's Aboriginal people.

Harper essentially buried the Kelowna Accord. Chief Stewart Phillip of the Union of B.C. Indian Chiefs lambasted the Conservatives for their failure to live up to the previous government's commitments. Shortly after the budget speech, he made the following pronouncement: "Today, Aboriginal people across Canada learned that Prime Minister Harper has a wooden heart to match his wooden smile."[2] Adding insult to injury, the PM had previously appointed Maurice Vallecott as chair of the Parliamentary Aboriginal Affairs Committee, in spite of allegations of his MP's bias against Aboriginal people.

Shortly afterwards, Mr. Vallecott falsely attributed a statement that judges "actually have these discerning and almost prophetic abilities to be able to come and know the mind of the public and they take on almost these godlike powers"[3] to Chief Justice Beverley McLachlin. Amidst pressure from the Liberals, the Canadian Bar Association, the Chief Justice of the Supreme Court and Aboriginal leaders, Vallecott voluntarily resigned from the committee. Prime Minister Harper simply distanced himself from his outspoken MP.

Mr. Harper finally met with Ontario's premier, Dalton McGuinty, for a brief meeting in Toronto. He then directly hastened to a provincial Conservative fundraiser and introduced John Tory, a Conservative MPP, as the next premier in Ontario. A definite slap to the face of the Ontario voters! In a subsequent meeting in Québec, the Prime Minister stated that he tries to stay out of provincial politics ... Doublespeak lives on!

Frank Luntz, a well-known U.S. Republican pollster, was a guest speaker at a Civitas Society meeting held in Ottawa (Mr. Harper has had a very close association with this group). Luntz was a key player in the landslide victory of Bush in 1994. He urged a group of notable Conservatives to investigate the Liberals and present whatever dirt they could find to Canadians as a re-election strategy. Mr. Luntz had met with Mr. Harper the previous day.[4]

Stephenocchio

In a small shop, in a smallish neighborhood,
an old man puzzled over a small block of wood.
"How shall I carve it, great care I must take,
if it's done right, a great puppet I'll make!"

He whittled and shaved with barely any rest,
as marionettes go, this would be his best.
At last he had finished, looked on it with joy,
his lined face smiled, "What a wonderful boy!"

On that very night with stars all aglow,
an angel named Preston from heaven did flow.
He swished his wand once, the puppet did rise,
It jumped to its feet, flashing steely blue eyes.

"I'm free, I'm free, what a wonderful surprise,
I promise to be honest, I'll never tell lies!"
He packed his knapsack and traveled coast to coast,
"I'll change this country," he firmly did boast.

"I'll be the perfect leader, just you wait and see,
I'll restore the meaning to democracy!"
He befriended Emerson on the B.C. coast,
But the first promise made ended up as dried toast.

Nose a little longer, he left for Quebec,
on his way there, McGuinty he would reject.
At a meeting next day he said, "Trust in me.
Provincial affairs aren't my cup of tea!"

His nose jerked forward, just a mere inch or two,
then swore that he was a Canadian true.
Civitas beckoned, Frank Luntz strategized,
took the Bush road and the land marginalized.

The more that he traveled, the more his nose grew.
"The Supreme Court I respect, this is so true.
To be checked by judges, a Liberal lot?
Why should I censure Maurice Vallecott?"

A puppet without soul made of warped green lumber,
the plans for Kyoto he had torn asunder.
The oil patch kid, urged by personal gain,
let his softwood blunder drift to his brain.

His honker stretched out to the Kelowna Deal.
"Trust me my good friends, my empathy is real."
One chief spoke out about his wooden smile,
A wooden heart matched his political guile.

The puppet danced on, the end too far from sight,
the strings that moved him kept safely out of sight.
The poor carpenter so loathed this fable,
so he chose next to build a simple end table.

Prime Minister Harper emerged from very limited and controlled exposure to the public and the media to make his first international trip to Afghanistan.

He left behind controversies over:

- inviting Liberal David Emerson into a Conservative Cabinet position with the resultant disenfranchisement of over 30,000 Vancouver-Kingsway voters
- the PMO's statement that Harper would be "loathe" to deal with the Ethics Commissioner's investigation of himself over the Emerson affair
- his appointment of Gordon O'Connor, a former military lobbyist, as the Minister of Defense
- Alberta's premier Ralph Klein's proposal for two-tier health care
- mounting protest against the eventual scrapping of the provincially approved National Day Care Agreements
- his overly obvious focus on potentially seat-lucrative Quebec
- the appointment of a non-elected individual, Michael Fortier, as a Senator
- and the Minister of Public Works, a very highly sensitive position, especially after the "Sponsorship Scandal."

This highly publicized trip set the standard for how the Prime Minister would handle difficult political situations: whenever the road gets tough, create a diversion. This strategy would be effective were it not for the very obvious juxtaposition of questionable decisions or actions with a positive and highly visible buffer, either in a press announcement just prior or closely subsequent to the questionable act.

Political Rhetoric (Spin Away)

Cut and run,
no more scrum.
Hear Stephen talk,
See Stephen walk.
See his John Wayne stance.
See Stephen smirk while he talks.
See his thumb up.
Hear the shutters click.
See Stephen fly the plane.
Hear Stephen's speech.
Hear him pledge,
"We will not cut and run.
It is not my way,
it is not Canada's way."

Oh, oh,
trouble back home.
Where is Stephen?
Where's the PM?
We have questions.
We need answers.
Shapiro is at bay.
And there is Klein's third way?
What about Fortier?
Pourquoi toujours Charest?
What about national day care?
Parents are upset everywhere.
What's this about the lobbyist,
O'Connor's long munitions list?
See Harper run,
See Harper cut and run.
Cut and run,
No more scrum.

At RCMP headquarters in Vancouver, Prime Minister Harper announced the introduction of new legislation coming the next spring that would impose severe penalties for those caught street racing. Chuck Cadman, the independent MP whose vote saved the Liberal government from a vote of non-confidence over its budget, had introduced a private member's bill that would have legislated stiffer penalties for street racing. Mr. Cadman died last year after a courageous battle with skin cancer.

The PM praised Mr. Cadman's work as well as that of his wife, who had continued to carry the torch for the changes. At the press conference, Harper stated, "We've been in regular contact with Donna Cadman during the drafting of the bill."[5] Mrs. Cadman said that was an exaggeration, that the PM had met with her for twenty minutes when she visited Ottawa for the inauguration of a skin cancer-screening programme in memory of her husband. She said that Harper had mentioned that the street racing legislation was coming, but she did not view this statement as consultation.

In Vancouver, a reporter asked the Prime Minister if he had invited Mrs. Cadman to attend the press conference. In his response, he mentioned that she was not a member of the government or a Conservative. In an interview with CTV's Mike Duffy, Mrs. Cadman said that she had not known about the meeting and showed obvious unhappiness that she had not been invited to attend.

It appears that Mr. Harper used this public announcement to enhance his image with the electorate; however, his *faux pas* spoke reams about the man behind the message.

Said the Spider to the Fly ...

"Oh, what a sticky web I weave," the stealthy spider said,
as innocent flies squirmed helplessly, trapped in their death bed.
"I choose a tasty victim when it's too weak to oppose,
when fate gives them a blow, my strength only grows."

"From the centre of my web, all vibrations pass my way,
my control is absolute, I'll give none of it away.
I may be ruthless but it's a way to survive,
Look at those scrumptious morsels, I sure do know how to thrive!"

Leaving Nature now, we move to the political scene,
where people are hardhearted and so appallingly mean.
Where spin takes on new meaning with the result much the same,
shrewd strategy substitutes heart in this cruel-hearted chess game.

Harper announced stringent penalties for the street racing crime,
praising Cadman's efforts to give the guilty much more time.
Lauded Cadman's widow for picking up her husband's fight,
he made his press pronouncement with sheer absolute delight.

A reporter asked if Mrs. Cadman had ever been invited,
wondering if this courageous widow had simply been slighted.
Flustered and uncertain as to the answer he should give,
Stephen responded: she's not even a Conservative.

Meanwhile returning to the arachnid's silky netting,
on a plump little abdomen, the spider was feting.
Let the warning flash about this insatiable beast,
if you're not very careful, you'll be a part of its feast.

S tephen Harper paid a surprise visit to our troops in Afghanistan, his first official trip abroad. Sporting a spiffy commander-in-chief-looking vest, he boldly addressed our soldiers. "There will be some who want to cut and run, but cutting and running is not my way and it's not the Canadian way."[6] Harper had a contented look on his face when he suggested that Canadians and members of the opposition parties who asked questions about the mission were not supporting the troops. This was an obvious and deliberate twist of reality meant to bolster his image and set the groundwork for his new style of governance with a minority: bullying.

Back in Canada, voters in Vancouver-Kingsway continued to fume over Harper and Emerson's debacle. Many felt that they were cutting, running and refusing to take responsibility for an action that had loudly slapped democracy in the face. One wonders if the Prime Minister will be so committed to our international role and image when it comes to the Kyoto Protocol.

The Bold and The Feckless

Stephen Harper flew to Afghanistan,
to support our troops, what a worldly man!
He stated his position,
then slammed the Opposition,
politicking in a war ravaged land.

Some critics say he's been trying to hide,
That criticism now he can deride!
He put reporters at bay,
S'long Vancouver-Kingsway,
Another bump on the road that he can ride.

1 6th International AIDS Conference or Northern Canada Photo Op? Photo Op or AIDS Conference? Hmmm …

Canada has once again faced embarrassment and humiliation on the world stage.

The AIDS Conference, which attracted large numbers of world experts in the field, health care workers, researchers and advocates along with many personally affected by this modern day plague, was a resounding success in spite of the bad taste left by Stephen Harper's refusal to put in an appearance.

Stephen Lewis, UN Special Envoy for HIV/AIDS to Africa, former US president Bill Clinton, and Melinda and Bill Gates were keynote speakers. As the top elected representative in government, it was incumbent upon our Prime Minister to stand up and share with the world Canada's commitment to help alleviate the suffering of millions of afflicted AIDS sufferers and their families. Instead, a tour of the far North, which could have been easily rescheduled or worked around, was his chosen priority. A cold excursion demonstrating what appeared to be an even colder nature!

Participants at the conference had hoped for an announcement about a Canada HIV/AIDS funding commitment, but the government's voice was noisily silent. Perhaps the bad publicity generated will push the Conservatives into action on this front. Health Minister Clement countered the request for a three year renewal of the Vancouver Safe Injection Site with a very short extension of funding and a call for more study in spite of existing research that validated its success in addiction counseling, prevention of overdosing and prevention of HIV/AIDS. The many Site supporters were vocally upset. "Further Study" has become a working tool of convenience in the arsenal of Conservative ideology.

Too Politicized

Twenty-five million, the death toll rings tragic,
AIDS now sits as the world's worst epidemic.
Thousands upon thousands lost souls every day,
Half innocent children who needlessly pay.

WHO suggests forty million live with HIV,
While nations lip-service the rising tragedy.
Stats provide convenient anonymity,
That serves to hide the face of anguished humanity.

Images of hospitals are full of the dying,
The air deeply fraught with tears of mute crying.
Secreted away, lepers left on a remote isle.
In a global asylum, their exile is vile.

Grandmothers raise children, orphanages are filled,
This horrific disease their parents has killed.
Newborns have arrived in this world all accursed,
Lives very fragile, time-destined for the worst.

Victims caught in a cycle of unrelenting pain,
While self-righteous bigots point fingers of blame.
Poverty and illness understandably tied,
Child Care providers slowly have died.

The illness rages while effluents grow fatter,
Moral issues are at stake but seem not to matter.
Medication would help but deemed too high a cost.
While governments quibble, and millions are lost.

A world AIDS summit, twenty-six thousand in all,
Went to Toronto and responded valiantly to the call.
Victims, advocates, caregivers, even scientists,
Gathered as one, along with philanthropists.

Stephen Lewis delivered a heartfelt discourse,
Clinton proved to be quite a catalytic force.
Melinda and Bill offered their financial weight,
But Harper chose absence, a moralist's mistake.

He received the invite soon after his election,
months later, at last, he shared his intention.
This "coarse" affair was by far "too politicized,"
He was quite busy, the media had advised.

Harper's excuse veered on the high side of sublime,
Instead ribbon-cutting at an Arctic diamond mine?
A cruise on a ship safeguarding our sovereignty?
Too far below a good Prime Minister's dignity.

At the conference all tuned in with wishful ears
"The safe injection site's fate? Please calm our fears!"
Research had concluded a drop in HIV.
Harper again deferred, instead sought a new study.

Humanists looked on in most indignant outrage,
At fossil ideas drawn from a dark age.
He had succumbed to such a self-righteous vanity,
Was simply blindsided to a distressed humanity.

S hortly after taking power, the Prime Minister enticed David Emerson to cross the floor, at the cost of democratic process, and appointed Michael Fortier to the Senate, making him the inaccessible Minister of Public Works, in spite of Harper's belief that senators should be publicly elected. He gagged his Cabinet Ministers, his backbenchers and senior civil servants. All announcements unrelated to his five-point plan had to first pass through the Prime Minister's office. He refused to announce the times of his Cabinet meetings and minimized the accessibility of the press to his Ministers. He disabled the traditional freedom of the Parliamentary Press to ask questions on behalf of Canadians.

He chose instead tightly controlled press announcements and selected the journalists who would ask the questions. He refused to present a list of election campaign contributors to the Ethics Commissioner. He scrapped the patronage review plan after the opposition members rejected Gwyn Morgan, his nominee for the chair of that committee. His party ignored rules of the Election Act during their 2005 campaign convention.

Transparency and accountability have taken on entirely new meanings in the "new" Canadian government.

Absolutely Clear

I want to make myself absolutely clear.

The Softwood Deal? I'll make the Yanks stick to the rules,
Make pulp of ugly cross-border duels!
Ceded a billion, Free Trade turfed somewhere in the woods,
Precedent for all other export goods.

Veterans' widows? I'll take good care of your needs,
I'll honour your spouses' valiant deeds.
Swore quick firm action, once in office changed his mind,
Elected to act in his own sweet time.

Let me make myself unequivocally clear,
Promises aren't always quite how they appear.

Transparency? My friends, I solemnly declare,
My deeds and my thoughts, I'll always lay bare.
Canada starved for news on APEC's meeting,
Soundly gave the free press one more beating.

Accountability? Now that's my cup of tea!
We'll be squeaky clean, just you wait and see.
Close to a million dollars, a convention gift,
The Election Act, given the short shrift.

Let me make myself unquestionably clear,
What you had thought you heard, you really didn't hear.

Honour our brave soldiers, support our troops abroad,
Their selfless courage, this we all applaud,
Our heroes flown back for sad repatriation,
Veiled from the eyes of a mourning nation.

Pensioners, my promise will give security,
Your golden years, just entrust them to me.
Changed the Income Trust rules, lives on a downhill run,
And the Tories' advice was go take a valium.

Let me make myself exceedingly clear,
Election words are cheap, actions are dear.

Human rights in China, a knight on a crusade,
Fight for the oppressed but forgive my tirade.
He let Aboriginals live in dire squalor,
And sold them out for the "almighty dollar."

Women's rights, this issue truly strikes home sweet home,
Your role is clearly blessed, your rights well known.
Scratched out the word "equality" from the mandate,
And made Status of Women a "guy's" mistake.

Let me make myself irrefutably clear.
Was that my real election promise? Oh dear!

I'm right on the right of rights. You get what I said?
Breach civil liberty? I'd rather be dead!
The Court Challenges Programme was quickly laid waste,
Constitutional rights were coldly defaced.

Fiscal imbalance I will personally solve,
A problem solver, I act with resolve.
The premiers growled and squabbled, fur and feathers flew,
Without a consensus, what could he do?

His new Canada would be a pleasant surprise,
Just keep the plan cached from all prying eyes,
With stealth and shrewd design, he'll effect his mission,
Great to be such a slick politician!

Want to I absolutely clear myself make!

The status and the aspirations of Quebecers have long simmered just below the surface of Canada's political waters, occasionally leaping dramatically into view, more recently in the form of Meech Lake, the Charlottetown Accord and two referendums, the last of which left both Canadian federalists and Quebec separatists flopping on shore, gasping for breath, so close was the outcome.

Last summer, Liberal leadership contender, Michael Ignatieff, toyed with the idea of recognizing Quebec as a nation, stimulating the Quebec wing of his party to formerly take the idea to their convention floor in Montreal. Enter Bloc leader, Gilles Duceppe, who planned to present a Commons motion to recognize Quebec as a nation. The Prime Minister strategically and summarily pre-empted Duceppe with a counter-proposal that the "Québécois form a nation within a united Canada."

Media fireworks, indignation, frustration, impassioned speeches, a Cabinet member's resignation, abstentions, spin and counter-spin, flying definitions of "nation" and "Quebecois," political manoeuvring and finally, self-congratulatory handshakes all around! After a brief debate, Harper's amendment passed with an overwhelming majority. When the dust settled, a nebulous and inflammatory motion that was wide open to interpretation floated carelessly throughout Canada.

Harper, in his indefatigable thirst for power, control and image making, had petulantly picked up the gauntlet tossed down by Duceppe and rushed himself and the country headlong into the reopening of the national debate on unity. Pierre Trudeau, one of Harper's most disliked political figures, would have avoided the game playing, allowed Duceppe's motion to be defeated by the House, then taken steps to counter the after-shock and ameliorate the situation.

A Question of Thrust

A strange calm spread throughout the Commons today,
The gallery was shocked, thought they missed the melee.
Instead they saw warm handshakes and pats on the back,
All those cross-the-floor smiles with no partisan attacks.

Disdain and hair slamming had become the common fare,
Shouting and hurling insults with teeth laid quite bare.
"You're a potted flower – no, you're a scurrilous dog!"
And the country tuned in all completely agog.

The fighting a disgrace, and questions left unanswered,
Or at best, surreptitiously deferred and never quite dealt with.
However, this day was an exception, the time to take note,
That proceedings had turned into a cheerless sad joke.

Michael Ignatieff caused ripe trepidation,
As he christened Quebec a birthright nation.
Old tremors had swiftly spread across the land,
As Sovereignty once again raised its strong fisted hand.

Liberals soon embraced his ripe emotion,
And set this idea into parliamentary motion.
It would be a question at the leadership debate,
But a political leg trap with no end but ill fate!

Gilles had sensed weakness and the wind was in his favor,
So he chose to add a pinch of sovereignist flavor.
He claimed "Quebec's a nation!" and put feds right on the spot.
And Harper fired back without giving a second thought.

Not one to pass up a boost to his fame
He chose to play the political game,
Knee jerk reactions in spite of the stakes,
Bad for a leader who's prone to mistakes.

Pre-empted the Bloc's pitch in reckless haste,
All sense of this issue quickly laid waste.
You're in Canada, said he with a gloat,
We'll see what happens when I call a vote!

The outcome he knew, the end count foreseen,
Two hundred and sixty-six to sixteen.
Shortly after this overwhelming win,
Each party ground out their victory spin.

The Tories, self-acclaimed for their quick action,
Claimed to have calmed this Quebecois faction.
"We're the champs of national unity,
We know best!" declared with impunity.

Leader Duceppe had the opposite take,
Official nationhood, what a huge break!
A nation within to nation without,
The distance between was not a far shout.

The Whigs cheered at their astonishing luck,
An apt chance to pass this unwanted buck.
No longer a dreaded election stress,
Neatly sidestepped a political mess.

Jack clicked his heels, sought the Francophone vote,
Saw new room in Quebec, he went for broke.
Dreamt entry to this elusive landscape,
Aspiring for a political break.

Quebecers watched in tense speculation,
First Nation eyed the fight with new tension.
Provinces questioned this proclamation,
Would they one day be a distinct nation?

The other francophones, what was their station?
Would they be part of this new formed nation?
Plenty of questions? The answers were few.
"Please share all with us, once you have a clue!"

"What does nationhood mean? What's a Quebecois?
What, no answer? *Je ne sais pas pourquoi!*"
The sixteen naysayers made a wise choice,
As they honed in to the Canadian voice.

He should have consulted First Officer Chong,
Who'd have steered him far from this risky wrong.
His ego blew canvas, sheets stretched too tight,
Captain Steve lost his way, sailed out of sight.

This farce had demanded a tough decision,
By a Prime Minister who has proactive vision.
To the floor the Bloc's motion should have gone,
Defeated it then, let the country move on.

It should be a challenging time for a Prime Minister who has had very limited overseas experience to take over Canada's Foreign Affairs' portfolio. Yet, PM Harper has charged ahead and decisively and immediately upon election implemented his untried theories, even before tackling home issues. In the process, he has parted company with previous leaders John Diefenbaker, Lester B. Pearson, Pierre Trudeau, Jean Chrétien and Paul Martin by aligning himself with George Bush, the Republican Party and their neo-conservative philosophy. His cozying up to Bush is reminiscent of Mulroney's alliance with U.S. President Reagan and the free-trade agreement struck between the two countries, which Harper effortlessly botched through his handling of the softwood lumber dispute. It is interesting to note that Harper's first official guest to Parliament was Australia's Conservative Prime Minister John Howard, who used our Parliament to praise the George Bush administration.

Whereas before Canada was viewed and respected internationally as a peacekeeper and a mediator, the country's new direction now smacks of a gunboat mentality. Harper was the first world leader to cut off funds that involved Hamas in the Palestinian authority in spite of the suffering that it would cause innocent, starving people. Hamas' goal to eliminate Israel is unacceptable, yet need the poor suffer for the decisions of their government?

In the 2006 conflict between Lebanon and Israel, many died, many were injured and thousands were displaced from their homes in both countries. Instead of referring to the Israeli response to cross-border attacks and kidnapping of a soldier as "measured," Harper and his Foreign Affairs department needed to work as an intermediary, a mediator who would work to help solve the crisis and attempt through diplomatic means to restore peace.

Meanwhile, the Prime Minister extended the Afghanistan mission by two years without a proper, democratic debate in Parliament. The process was unequivocally a sham. Harper stated that he would never desert the families of our soldiers who have died in Afghanistan by ending the mission. His approach at home is like his approach abroad: 'You're either with me or against me.' Doesn't that remind you of someone of medium height and somewhat bushy in appear-

72

ance? By *George,* you've guessed it! You either support the mission as it exists or you are not supporting our soldiers. Nothing could be further from the truth.

In spite of his uncalled for admonitions, Canadians will forever honour those who gave their lives fighting for democracy and for Canada. However, a leader should never be so rigid as to not tolerate questions about the mission that not only affects our remaining soldiers but also Canada's principles. We need only look at the US war in Iraq and Bush's dogmatic insistence that they have done the right thing in spite of the chaos and massive loss of life in that country. In opposition at the time, Harper supported the Iraqi mission in 2003. Had Harper been in power at the time of the invasion, would our soldiers be there, suffering great losses as the Americans are?

One also wonders about the PM's extreme lack of diplomacy with China. Does he know nothing about the importance of face when dealing with other countries, especially China? If you can't get in the front door, you might just as well save your breath when promoting human rights. At the APEC Summit in Hanoi, Vietnam, Chinese President Hu eventually gave Harper fifteen minutes of his time. Harper was lucky to get even that. It's pretty challenging to affect change in the thinking of the leader of a country that will eventually surpass the U.S. as a world powerhouse.

Harper's action with respect to the Kyoto Protocol is a disgrace. Canada held a leadership role in rallying countries into a world organization that would take the initiative to face the climate change process. His rejection of Canada's commitments to Kyoto has undoubtedly watered down the resolve of some countries and exacerbated the climate-related crises that have already occurred in Africa.

Harper's learning curve on the international scene seems unattainably high and his initial performance forebodes an unprecedented change to our traditional and successful approach to world politics.

A Fable

A youthful traveler roamed across the vast land,
A sling and several rocks grasped tightly in hand.
"I seek out evil, I'm on a moral crusade,
I'll fight human rights' abuses, so don't be afraid!"

The world seemed a strange place and he felt all alone,
For he'd never before trekked so far from his home.
He had read all the books, was a scholarly man,
Yet what he saw amazed him, his learning was a sham.

To Afghanistan he strode, his heart it did sing
He secured a true stone in the pouch of his sling.
"You've not before lived in a democratic state,
I'll pummel you to accept, just yield to your fate."

The ancient warlords watched, unmoved by his speech,
History had passed down, they were out of his reach.
For freedom imposed by a sling cannot endure,
A change over time is the sole natural cure.

Saddened but not beaten, he set his sights anew,
Traveled to the Orient and sought Emperor Hu.
Several months later stood before the Great Wall,
Brandishing his weapon, he let out a strident call:

"Heed my words, I am a force to be reckoned with,
That size determines strength is nothing but a myth.
Respect your subjects' rights, you must employ good sense!"
His words ricocheted back and left a chilling silence.

Stonewalled once more, now leery of the dragon beast,
He set his course by compass and trudged to the Mid-East.
The first sight his eyes embraced were rivers of red,
The fields littered with bodies of the innocent dead.

"A measured response, the reason is truly just!"
Bodies of both warring tribes lay rotting in the dust.
A mourner overheard, asked why he failed to grieve,
"If you can't help us find peace, you might as well leave!"

For Palestine he left, undaunted by coldness,
Still mightily impressed by his self-serving boldness.
In all directions he witnessed untenable mess,
Of unbridled poverty and abject distress.

Stroked his pouch of gold coin, felt its substantial weight,
Knew that he had the power to transform their fate.
Chose instead to punish their chiefs' evil intent,
Threw his hands up, to the darkest continent he went.

There, widespread famine and drought he soon met,
The village elders blamed the change in the climate.
Downcast, the traveler renounced his sad crusade,
But scurried back home and let his bad memories fade.

The moral of this fable, be careful abroad,
For the best laid plans can be absolutely flawed.
When an untried leader assumes complete control,
And makes bad decisions, it's his head that will roll.

ENDNOTES

1. Gwyn, Richard. "Steely PM taking Canada down a radical path." The Toronto Star, 02 May 2006.

2. "Union of B.C. Indian Chiefs Responds to Prime Minister Harper's Federal Budget" ubcic.bc.ca. <http://www.ubcic.bc.ca/News_Releases/UBCICNews05020601.htm>

3. "Vellacott resigns aboriginal post." GlobeandMail.com. 10 May 2006. <http://www.theglobeandmail.com/servlet/story/RTGAM.20060510. wvelacott0510/BNStory/National/home>

4. "Dig Up Dirt on Grits to Keep Power, Republican strategist tells Tories." Canada.com. 08 May 2006. <http://www.canada.com/saskatoonstarphoenix/news/national/story.html?id=a8595986-b7ec-498b-a352-65479e5c56f0>

5. "Harper to put brakes on street racing." Canada.com. 26 May 2006. <http://www.canada.com/edmontonjournal/news/story.html?id=8cd28f9c-517f-4e14-b1cb-d2f8af06b02>

6. "Canada committed to Afghan mission, Harper tells troops." CBC.ca. 13 March 2006. <http://www.cbc.ca/world/story/2006/03/13/harper_afghanistan060313.html>

CHAPTER THREE

WHO CAN PREDICT
THE WEATHER ANYWAY?

Man makes a death which Nature never made.
Edward Young

The ozone hole over the Antarctic may soon set the record
as being the world's biggest hole. This is the first year that
the world's biggest hole will not be a head of state.
Rick Mercer

Mark Tushingham, a scientist for Environment Canada, published a science fiction novel entitled *Hotter than Hell*, a work based on the world threat of global warming. Mr. Tushingham was scheduled to speak at a release engagement at the National Press Club in Ottawa on Thursday, April 13th, 2006. However, he received an e-mail from his superiors cautioning him not to attend the meeting and to cancel TV and radio interviews related to his book's release.

It had just been announced that the "new" government was scrapping fifteen climate change projects. During the same week, Prime Minister Harper presented his Accountability Act aimed at improving transparency and accountability in government. The PM had vowed to provide "iron-clad" protection to whistleblowers who would dare to stand up and expose wrongdoing in the government. When asked about the silencing of the scientist, the Prime Minister responded that he wasn't aware of the details and "... I not only hope, but expect, that all elements of the bureaucracy will be working with us to achieve our objectives."[1] Actions certainly speak louder than easy campaign words.

Mr. Harper had previously informed all members of his caucus and senior bureaucrats that public announcements, outside of those related to his five-point plan, had to first be approved by the Prime Minister's Office. One wonders how, in such a tightly controlled environment, he wasn't aware of the details of the Tushingham censorship caper. Canadians have noticed many discrepancies and inconsistencies in Mr. Harper's new and hardly fresh approach to politics.

Ironically, as a result of receiving a resounding public response to the undemocratic muzzling of its author, DreamCatcher publisher Elizabeth Margaris indicated that the book would go into a second printing and that a Canadian company was interested in purchasing TV and film rights. She expressed her gratitude that Environment Canada and then-Environmental Minister Rona Ambrose had indirectly brought public attention to the novel and to the global warming issue.

Temperature Rising

"Stand up for Canada, a new era we guarantee,
to voters we pledge absolute accountability.
Transparency we will take to the ultimate level,
in our integrity, all Canadians will revel!

The Liberals are all shysters, dishonest to the core.
The Sponsorship Scandal, do we need to say more?
We will save Canada with our Accountability Act!
All "whistleblowers" we'll also safeguard, now that is a fact."

Their propaganda machine raged from sea to land to sea,
a minority government the Tories would soon be.
Once in power, the mask was quickly cast away,
as Harper embezzled David from Vancouver-Kingsway.

The PM had promised all the new senators by vote,
then appointed Fortier, an unelected standing joke.
Steve made him Public Works Minister, stashed him aside,
unaccountably absent, transparency defied.

A federal scientist dared to pass on a warning,
by writing a novel that focused on global warming.
The novel's debut created outrageous discord,
for the Tories were busy smothering the Kyoto Accord.

"Cancel the book meeting and all will be fine,
all levels of bureaucracy must follow party line!"
With one quick memo, another promise not kept.
Whistleblowers take close heed, lest your future be wrecked.

In May 2006, six Canadian-based environmental groups asked then-Environment Minister Rona Ambrose to resign as president of the Kyoto talks in Bonn, Germany, to save Canada from worldwide ridicule. They, along with many Canadians, were shocked when the Conservative government quietly and dramatically cut a large number of the country's environmental programs, substituting as its major strategy a costly and relatively ineffective approach that would give tax credits to public transit users.

Critics stated Ambrose had abandoned the Kyoto Protocol, its approximately 190 participating countries and Canada's legal international commitment when she declared that it would be impossible for Canada to meet Kyoto targets. She suggested that to do this, every plane, train and automobile would need to be removed from the landscape: "... we would have to pull every truck and car off the street, shut down every train and ground every plane ... To reach our Kyoto target, we have to shut off all the lights and shut down the entire agriculture industry."[2] Many dismissed these as nonsensical statements that simply blurred the feasibility of meeting targets with the appropriate domestic approach. Canada's environment guru, David Suzuki, publicly lambasted the Conservatives for their unconscionable stance.

One of the objectives of the two week meeting in Germany was to develop the second phase of the Kyoto agreement and to enlist additional developing countries to sign on to the plan with a commitment to reduce greenhouse gas emissions. The Environment Minister was greeted in Bonn with yet another petition, this time from 300 worldwide, non-governmental environmental groups, also asking her to resign as chairperson.

Ambrose opened the meeting, requested a softening of the targets for Canada, then cut and ran back to Canada two days later. Once again, Frank Luntz, the U.S. Republican pollster and advisor who has a telling association with Stephen Harper and the Conservative Party, is strongly influencing Canadian policy, this time on the environment. Like Luntz and Bush, the new government questions why we should get on board with Kyoto requirements when India and China have not.

The answer to that is simple. Let Canada continue to serve as a good example of a concerned, committed and responsible country that is willing to tackle head-on the dangers implicit in global warming and climate change.

Alberta's Tar Sands produce a quality of oil that creates the most greenhouse gases. One would assume that this would be one industry requiring regulation. However, according to a 2005 report by *Oxford Analytica,* the Alberta Energy and Utilities Board estimated that there are 1.6 trillion barrels of crude oil in the Tar Sands. With current high prices, they also predicted that 175 billion barrels could be recoverable. This raised Canada's oil reserves from about 5 billion to 180 billion barrels, second only to Saudi Arabia. The Board also forecasted that by 2015, Canadian exports of crude oil would almost double to 2.8 million barrels per day.[3]

With China's strong interest in the Tar Sands, the U.S. is concerned that they will lose a cheap and reliable source of oil – a situation that Washington deems to be a strategic threat. Enter the NAFTA Agreement, with its U.S. guaranteed access to Canadian oil, and Harper's American style of voluntary regulation of emissions. The Alberta-based federal government is naturally giving the Tar Sands a sidelong wink.

Rona in
Ambroseland

I'm late, too late, for a very unsavory date.
Kyoto calls, too many catcalls,
I'm late, too late, I'm late.
I'm late and when I waver,
I lose the cool I savor.
My fuzzy words and climate calls,
Put me out of everyone's favor.
I talk and then I whine, whine, whine,
I wish that I could lie.
There's danger if I do not stop,
There'll be a world outcry.
I'm overdue, in a climate stew.
Can't even say I'll try.
I'm late, it's fate!
Oh my, oh me, oh my!

I'm late, too late, oh what a horrible, icky fate.
No time to plan or get a tan,
I'm late, too late, I'm late.
I'm late and when I speak, environmentalists freak.
Turn out your lights, get out and walk,
The future's not that bleak!
I spin and then I point, point, point,
I wish that I could lie.
There's danger if I dare to speak
And here's the reason why.
I'm very new, on Harper's crew.
Can't even say I'll try.
I'm late, it's fate!
Oh my, oh me, oh my!

I'm late, too late, for a cute Kyoto remake.
Just time to scrap, I'm in a flap,
I'm late, too late, I'm late.
I'm late and when I whine,
They ask me to resign.
My Bushy hair and speaking flair,
It all takes too much time.
A Canadian plan I'll make, make, make,
I wish that I could lie.
The polar ice melts, I dare not stop,
Stephen tells me why.
Our western fans support Tar Sands.
I know that I must try.
I'm late, its fate!
Oh my, oh me, oh my!

I'm late, too late, must fix this Kyoto mistake.
No time to lead or even take heed,
Too late, too late, too late.
Please accept this transit pass,
Reduce our greenhouse gas.
Global warming? Climate control?
These words we must bypass.
I close my eyes, then flop, flop, flop,
I wish that I could lie.
Why shouldn't I chair Kyoto,
here's the reason why.
We're neat, we're sweet, we're the oil elite.
Why should I even try?

I'm late, it's fate!
Oh my, oh me, oh my!

A document leaked to the press indicated that the Conservative government was not only backtracking on the legally binding, international Kyoto agreement, but also was undermining its proactive spirit.

One part of the instructions given to Canada's Kyoto negotiators stated that, "Canada will not support agreement on language in the work program that commits developed countries to more stringent targets in the future." Canada's then-Environment Minister Rona Ambrose stated, "... we support the two-year assessment that is going to commence after the meetings in Bonn." She added that any new agreement "...must include the USA," a comment that highlighted the Conservative government's penchant for the policy of our southern neighbors. [4]

With respect to Canada's largest emitters of greenhouse gases, the Pembina Institute indicated that for the cost of twelve cents to thirty-four cents per barrel of oil, all of the oil companies could be using current emission reducing technologies. With their current high levels of profit, one would assume that if this were a legal requirement, they would be, at least, somewhat philosophical about their compliance.

Nine Minutes and Counting

An ominous destiny should Nature's wrath unfurl,
now that global warming threatens our vulnerable world?
The leaders of our country bow to industry demands,
ignoring blatant dangers like the Alberta Tar Sands.

From Convention on Climate Change to Kyoto Accord,
the world's cleverest politicians chose to climb on board.
Canada took the lead in a worldwide approach,
while the U.S. waffled and garnered scientific reproach.

Harper thought like Bush and sent Rona Ambrose to Bonn
to chair Kyoto, and hope for our environment was gone.
Spoke out for nine minutes, said she'd need two years to assess,
Then scurried back home leaving Protocol in a mess.

The reputation of our country lay torn and tattered,
Our long, proud tradition had been seriously battered.
Sabotage intimated, a Tory document leak,
the destruction of Kyoto, great damage they would wreak.

Bad publicity thus pushed Conservatives into action,
frantically hoping to counter public reaction.
What could they bring forward to cover their intentions,
and rescue their Party from this critical attention?

Of course, the usual spin about the last thirteen years,
that same worn out record, now very boring to the ears.
Stephen Harper, blinded by steely ironfisted will,
boldly built his ivory fortress on Parliament Hill.

An opportunity missed to lead the world in this plan,
when it comes to the environment, they don't give a damn.
Where are they taking us, more importantly at what cost?
Time for decisive action before the planet is lost.

In a from-the-hip reflex action, Prime Minister Harper and then-Environmental Minister Rona Ambrose announced a plan to mandate five percent ethanol in gasoline by 2010. The Conservatives had been floundering in their effort to counteract domestic and international criticism of sabotaging the Kyoto Protocol and slashing existing Canadian environmental programmes without a viable replacement plan. Many viewed the announcement as a smokescreen that simply added to the polluted atmosphere.

Using ethanol in fuel, still a questionable minor step, cannot take the place of needed comprehensive measures to control greenhouse gas emissions. The processing, growing and harvesting of the corn as well as the transportation of the new fuel (it cannot be shipped by pipeline) requires more energy than what it produces. Prices at the pump would be higher and the fuel would burn at about three quarters of the efficiency, thereby upping the cost to the consumer. On the taxpayer front, the corn industry takes the lead in North America as one of the most heavily subsidized. EnerGuide, which the Conservatives ruthlessly cut, was a more immediate and cost-effective programme of greenhouse gas reduction.

Corn Bob and Steve, Eh?

It was a quiet day on the farm, two old friends a rockin',
it weren't too very long before they all commenced a talkin'.
"Cuzzin Steve, whatch ya think about this durn Kyoto thing,
and global warming and all the troubles they says it'll bring?"

"Now, Corn Bob, don't you start a frettin' about that stuff,
all this dang talk about climate change is more than enough!
You see, the science's a country mile from being verified,
so on this questionable issue, my good time I will bide."

"Until then I'll have to divert my voters' attention,
and hide all that durn environmentalists' dissension.
Corn Bob, with your help I reckon I can do it all,
just plant some more corn, we'll turn it into ethanol!"

"Hot diggity dang, cuzzin' Steve, you're as slick as a pig!
Shazam! Ain't no wonder ya got to be someone big!"
Steve spat twice on the veranda floor then flashed a broad grin,
"Ain't no problem too big … just gotta give it the right spin!"

"My Alberta oil cuzzins won't mind this compromise,
if that durn old profit killer Kyoto Accord dies.
Canadians will think that I am very progressive,
even though this corny programme is downright recessive."

Steve rocked obsessively, totally absorbed in himself,
while cuzzin' Bob dreamt about millions of acres of wealth.
"I don't know how this country survived before I ran it,
it's much simpler when you ignore the needs of the planet."

W hile visiting on July 15th with British Prime Minister Tony Blair, Stephen Harper announced Canada as the up-and-coming energy superpower and the country that offers the most attractive international investment opportunities in the energy field. He spoke of the potential of Alberta's Tar Sands, denounced by many as an untamed, environmental cesspool and often mentioned in the same breath as the need for tight regulation of industrial CO_2 emissions. Criticism at home flared over the need to safely secure Canada's present and future energy needs before doling out and committing even more of our precious resources to energy hungry countries.

During the spring session of Parliament, opposition parties felt constant frustration over the Conservatives' international backtracking from the Kyoto Protocol and the cutting of research funds and environmental programmes without offering a viable replacement strategy. The Conservatives appeared to be scrambling to slap together an environmental programme for the fall session, an eight-month lag of relative inaction costly to the health of our planet.

The CO_2's Out of the Bag

With severe climactic change and rapid temperature rising,
world scientists issued a grim global warning.
When even Frank Lutz, Bush's secret PR guru,
recognized the danger, he at last changed his view.
The world was in amazement at Canada's new approach,
with a blasé government that was beyond all reproach.

Research mercilessly slashed, as parched grass to hungry scythe,
the wise lamented as they saw effective programmes die.
A Canada-made solution, what more could be wished for?
Commuter credits, ethanol plan … hey - you want some more?
Ambrose ridiculed for her pre-recorded lines,
a skill perfected under Meister King Ralph Klein.

When queried, Harper smiled, widely purred, a cool Cheshire cat,
his non-answers polished with shrugging motion down pat.
Don't question our plans for the future, just look at the past,
while scientists asked how long this rhetoric could last.
The tipping point edged closer, the northern ice caps shrinking,
underscoring the PM's faulty lame thinking.

When S.J. Harper stepped abroad en route to the G-8,
in "jolly old" proclaimed himself a new oil sheik.
In a flash, the Cheshire Cat boldly leapt from the sac,
sharp claws bared, landing square on the poor environment's back.
Flaunting the Tar Sands as a world-available resource,
all then understood why he lacked a planet remorse.

Beware of the "noble lie," the Straussian message,
meant to mislead and make your deep anxieties diminish.
Behind each action there lies a well-calculated plan,
Aided and abetted by the press gallery ban.
Judge each action and the underlying motivation,
stand proud and keep in sight the essence of our nation.

A former chief World Bank economist, Sir Nicholas Stern, released a government-sponsored report on August 30, 2006, stating that if we were to immediately cut greenhouse gas emissions, the cost would only be 1% of the gross domestic product every year.[5] If the world collectively does not take action in the immediate future, the resultant recession would cost 20% of the GDP. This should, indeed, be a stern warning to our Prime Minister, who was educated as an economist.

Since scientific reason has not prevailed in the government's environmental plan (perish the thought that they should use the term "global warming"), then perhaps the "almighty dollar" will turn their heads - hit them where it hurts! Concerns about the fate of humanity and the survival of our planet have, to date, had very little effect.

The report calls for a collective worldwide response to this impending disaster. The Canadian government's sabotage of the Kyoto Protocol vilifies her reputation as a caring and responsible nation. It's time for a serious Green Plan!

A Stern Warning

An economist speaks, the world takes heed,
action will happen when it involves greed.
Climate change threatens, the time is to act,
the board rooms speak out, there's no going back.

Check out our oceans' depleted resources,
in forty years, the end of our food sources.
Canada wavers, always faltering,
this time standing behind bottom trawling.

The Hot Air Act, not so very nifty,
shifted the goal to year 2050.
Petulantly, Tories huff and they puff,
scientists cry: you're not doing enough!

Harper cancelled his next EU meeting,
his Kyoto tactic would get quite a beating.
In Nairobi, discussions of our earth's fate.
And Ambrose arrived, unfashionably late.

Why take Natives or those scientific folk,
with a Clean Air Act that's a standing joke?
Why tint this act with tree hugger sorrow?
Harper can't guess the weather tomorrow!

After months of dithering and the cancellation of existing environmental programmes followed by routine announcements that there would soon be an announcement of a new environmental plan, the Conservatives' "Made in Canada" Clean Air Act was finally tabled in the Commons on October 19, 2006. On that day, the "new" government virtually sealed its abandonment of the legally binding Kyoto Protocol that called for a reduction of green house gas emissions to 6% below the 1990 levels of emissions.

With the Act's "Notice of Intent" reference, there would be government consultation with industrial greenhouse gas emitters to be completed by 2010. Targets would be established for 2010 to 2015 with additional targets to be set in 2020. For those of us who should live that long, there will be a projected 45 to 60% reduction by 2050 based on 2003 levels instead of 1990 levels. Don't hold your greenhouse gas-filled breath for a significant change in many present Canadians' lifetime!

The existing Canadian Environmental Protection Act has the power to immediately affect necessary strategies to set desperately needed short-term goals without the lengthy process of establishing new legislation to do the same job. And now the kicker: enter the term "intensity based targets" which do not put a cap on greenhouse gas emissions. Rather, as long as an industry is permitted to increase the production of its product, emissions will continue to rise higher. The Kyoto plan wins hands down!

In November of 2006, Environment Minister Ambrose made a perfunctory appearance at the Kyoto Summit in Nairobi, Africa, an ironic location for her to make a social call when the people of Africa are experiencing a savage increase in killer droughts and will continue to be the most victimized by global warming. Prime Minister Harper needs to come to grips with his responsibility in dealing with global warming.

Global Terrorists

An old man lazily straddled a bench near the street,
Skin shrunk mercilessly in harsh dry heat.
When in the distance there arose a spewing dust cloud.
A rumbling engine grew more and more loud.
Sensing grave danger, instincts honed in like a knife,
His spine shivered tightly, sensed danger to life.

A half ton turned sharply, swerved fearlessly into sight,
Adrenaline pumped, pushing muscle into flight.
Men, women and children scattered in sheer abject fright,
Insurgents were screaming in feral delight.
Pungent puffs of thick, black smoke wafted up from the tail,
As rebels churned out a bullet-filled trail.

Stinking of oil, wide eyes bulged with uncontrolled lust,
Leapt down in defiance, boots on the dust.
The motley horde of rogues encircled their lieutenant,
A woman immersed in evil intentions.
In soft-spoken words, El Ronada gave the command:
Wreak cruel havoc on this destitute land.

Wipe out their water, obliterate every crop,
Spread disease and famine, striking non-stop.
Black hair glistening and swaying, she led the onslaught,
So what if Africa became too hot!
The marching orders for their crusade were quite exact,
Cast aside that mad global warming pact.

The old and the very young are as always the first,
To die from sheer famine and painful thirst.
Dengue fever struck hard, malaria took its toll,
Their bones spread out in a deadly dust bowl.
Their parched wailing spread unanswered across a bleak land,
Then was heard in the wind by Kofi Annan.

The general swiftly dealt with this inhumane pillage,
And diplomacy lost out to morality's outrage.
His blue helmeted soldiers hastily sniffed them out,
Followed the trail of the most recent drought.
El Ronada was nonplused, unashamed to the last,
As she laid the blame on old governments past.

Fearful for their lives, the scurrilous gangsters took flight,
And Africans cheered, at last rid of that blight.
El Ronada still claimed victory, a "measured" gain,
Stood by her belief, would strike once again.
Accounts of the skirmish spread both at home and abroad,
Her country's accords were rampant with fraud.

An image discoloured, a shattered reputation,
A challenging time, for a proud nation.

S tep One

The Prime Minister, as expected, announced the shuffling of his Cabinet. There had been major floundering in two portfolios that, Harper realized, was negatively impacting the Conservatives in the polls. Being the fine strategist that he is, he undoubtedly felt the announcement early in the New Year would symbolically show Canadians that the "new" government was making a "new" start, which was definitely needed. Canadians, however, realized that the PM's leadership style was top-down and new faces did little to camouflage the man behind every policy made and action taken.

Step Two

Stephen Harper selected the President of the Treasury Board, John Baird, to replace Ambrose in the environment portfolio. Mr. Baird brings along some unpleasant baggage, not only from his time as a MPP for the Mike Harris government in Ontario, but also from his brief stint as Treasury Board President. Shortly after his appointment, the new Minister appeared in a TV interview on the program *CBC Sunday,* and failed to give, when directly asked by host Carole MacNeil, one specific action that he would take to reduce greenhouse gases. He spoke of 'further consultation' that the Conservatives have already talked about for a year. When asked about Kyoto, Baird indicated that the protocol was struck many years ago and the government wanted a fresh start. As a MPP in Ontario, he had opposed Kyoto. Although asked again and again about his specific plans, he simply employed his usual tactic during Question Period in the Commons: attack the previous government's record and sidestep substantive responses.

Baird indicated the government had been busy with their priorities, very strongly suggesting that the environment was not an important issue. Enough time had been wasted. Canadians want action, not rhetoric. Global warming is the planet's most pressing issue. It cannot be shouted away.

Step Three

With superb Stephen Harper-timing and a speech that made the PMO beam with pride, former Liberal MP Wajid Khan told the media about his defection to the Conservative Party. Mr. Khan suggested that new Liberal Party Leader Stéphane Dion's alleged ultimatum forced him to decide between Canada and being a Liberal. In the old days, there would have been at least one hardball question from the press, such as " ....did Khan discuss crossing the floor with the PM prior to Dion taking over the Liberal leadership?" For the sake of democracy, all politicians who wish to change parties during their term should face a by-election in their riding. Emerson and now Khan have disenfranchised too many Canadian voters. After viewing the press conference, there is little question that long ago, Stephenocchio morphed from marionette to puppet master.

The Stevie Wonder Three-Step

An astounding thing happened on the Hill today,
Not shuffles or fluffles or MPs gone astray.
Yes, a change was effected in the Cabinet,
But the surprise came in words never spoken yet.

Baird beamed, this new environmental post the best,
A promotion hard earned, won by his yelling zest.
His skill at non-answers earned his boss's respect,
With his "past thirteen years" jab, he'd always deflect.

Was it Harper's words that Baird was his right hand man?
No, all knew the PM was an admiring fan.
After all, Baird helped with the billion-dollar cut.
On the vulnerables' backs, his status shot up.

Stephen valued his unrelenting dedication,
to change the law on political donation.
Perchance, a part of his minion's seduction,
His naught to sixty record was screaming corruption

Surely not words about Baird's enviro past,
Although the dearth there left most scientists aghast.
Perhaps it was his words about the Ottawa light rail?
His interference there caused a green plan to derail.

Was it stories about his Three Musketeer days,
with Flaherty and Clement and that Mike Harris phase?
No, it's better to leave these brutal tales untold,
Those times of wine and roses had quickly turned cold.

The parting of pawn Ambrose, well hardly a shock,
She obeyed Harper's commands, just a sheep in his flock.
When Harper at last heeded the voters' outcry,
Loyal Rona paid the price and was hung out to dry.

Finley was plucked from Social Development,
Botched up child day care, the PM had been hell bent.
Harper's cunning shift stirred hardly an emotion,
So what caused all that wild flurry of commotion?

Was it Stephen's praise of Ambrose? What had he meant
When he said she'd done "...a great deal for the environment."
No, it couldn't be that, that'd draw a nation wide laugh,
They'd only say he'd made another inane gaff!

Was it Khan's defection that created such a shock,
No, he picked Harper long ago, that was old talk.
His speech well orchestrated, words not at all new,
Flawlessly gave a speech, the common party blue.

Then why all the to-do about what had been said?
Harper had twigged in, scared his career would be dead.
Not for conviction but votes, his act was alarming,
He let his man Baird first use the words "global warming."

During Question Period on January 31, 2007, Opposition Party members confronted Stephen Harper with a letter he had written five years previously in which he had denounced the Kyoto Protocol.[6] When asked to personally rescind his statements, the Prime Minister would not do so; rather, he parried that the government believed in climate change. Canadians would have felt much more comfortable had he said he was wrong in the letter and that he would do absolutely everything in his power to deal with the climate change and global warming crisis.

Canada's "new government" initiated the release of American-style attack ads against the credibility of Stéphane Dion's past environmental record. The Conservatives even purchased prime television time during the Super Bowl. Most Canadians found it distasteful to incorporate this American political campaign strategy and are even more troubled that it occurred when an election had not even been called. Most would prefer that the PM give less credence to an undesirable political ideology that thrives south of the 49th parallel.

On February 2, 2007, the Intergovernmental Panel on Climate Change in Paris issued a gloomy prediction about the planet's future. Renown environmental scientists warned that even if the world completely eliminated greenhouse gas emissions by 2100, which in itself seems an impossibility, four centuries would pass and there would still be twice as much CO_2 in the atmosphere than what had existed at the beginning of the Industrial Revolution near the end of the 18th Century. Human activity, they stated, has created the majority of global warming since 1950. The consequences have been wild unpredictable weather, extreme drought and floods, severe wildfires and endangered plant and animal life. If emissions are not curbed by 2100, Greenland's ice sheet could melt and the depth of the oceans could rise by more than 6 m. Sea levels could rise 17 to 59 cm. The global temperature could rise as much as 6° Celsius by 2100.[7] Life as we know it today would cease to exist.

The only hope is immediate and comprehensive action that will require absolute conviction on the part of the world's leaders. To not face up to the threat is criminal.

Smearenuf Cocktail Americano

Blue smoke seductively swirling, words purging from tight lips.
you know, those pithy, spontaneous gems and acid-tipped quips
that sheer and slander that derisively mock,
barbed jabs that rise amidst unguarded talk.

Time spun full circle, recalled thoughts of ancient passage rites,
invoking primal instincts, Wrestlemania! and boxing fights,
warrior blood baths, you know what I mean,
while the clan crouched by the big TV screen.

The Super Bowl beckoned, that cherished gridiron melee
where muscle-chiseled athletes engaged in a wild foray,
as millions looked on, swilling their icy brew
with eyes latched on the plays like crazy glue.

The backroom boys expectant, sticky red blood soon to flow,
while they thrilled at their ringer firing off a stunning blow
shouting "Here's a drink that'll beat our green foe,
Smearenuf Cocktail, Americano!"

Flaming Arrow Flanagan whooped and Deadeye Brodie cheered
as mudslinger Frankie Luntz and Wilkins cackled and sneered
and Wilson rasped out in total delight
when Fortier at last rolled into sight.

Pigskin sliced through the air, the long-awaited match had begun,
host announcing "The commercial's on soon, who has more fun!"
Feeling tipsy, pouring all one more drink,
then bellowed, "Dion's green image will shrink!"

The new cocktail flowed freely, play-by-play action blurring
with loud raucous laughter and animated speech slurring,
then a shout "Here is our million-dollar ad,
great to be so plush. Hey Kingsley, so sad!"

While staggering and hollering, whistling and slapping backs,
national proof of their best shrewdest campaign ad attacks
flashed on, then the host called all to order,
praised this tactic used south of the border.

Emotions rampaged, soared up to a roller coaster high,
but as oft happens at wild parties, one started to cry,
shocking the horde with his steely-eyed tears
that brought to the surface all their worst fears.

He babbled about a money sucking socialist scheme,
Kyoto, that'd cripple the gas and oil industry dream,
wailed CO_2 is essential to life,
emission control would lead to dire strife.

Canada's green man Brian tried to stem the host's tears,
reassure the backroom lads, quell their unexpected fears,
asked his protégé to buck up and be strong
and admit his climate change views were absolutely wrong.

The words barely spoken, host regaining self-possession,
then dried crocodile tears, affirmed his climate confession
asserting "I'll never change what I believe,
if you doubt my view, I'd like you to leave!"

The party ended with Colts and Bears thrashing on the field
with the backroom boys terrified that their fate had been sealed
by the resolve of their proud and precocious chief
who cared squat about the world's impending grief.

ENDNOTES

1. "Minister Stops Book Talk by Environment Canada Scientist." CBC.ca. 13 April 2006. <http://www.cbc.ca/arts/story/2006/04/13/ambrose-climate. html>

2. "Speaking Notes for an Address by the Honourable Rona Ambrose, Minister of the Environment of Canada." ec.gc.ca. 11 May 2006. <http://www. ec.gc.ca/minister/speeches/2006/060511_s_e.htm>

3. "Canada to compete in oil market." Forbes.com. 17 February 2005. <http:// www.forbes.com/energy/2005/02/17/cz_0217oxan_canadaoil.html>

4. "Environmentalists say Canada undermines Kyoto" Reuters.com. 22 May 2006. <http://uk.news.yahoo.com/22052006/325/environmentalists-say-canada-undermines-kyoto.html>

5. "Bleak warning on warming: Solving problem will require 1% of global GDP Report." trca.on.ca. 30 October 2006. <http://www.trca.on.ca/hot_ issues/?articleID=1161>

6. "Harper blasted Kyoto in 2002 fundraising letter." CTV.ca. 20 January 2007. <http://www.ctv.ca/servlet/ArticleNews/story/CTVNews/20070130/ harper_kyoto_070130/20070130>

7. Borenstein, Seth. ""We're just going to have to live with it," top U.S. scientists say." Toronto Star. 02 February 2007.

CHAPTER FOUR

SO THIS IS A NEW DEMOCRACY …?

The silence of a wise man is always meaningful.
Leo Strauss, Thoughts on Machiavelli

I've got more control now. I'm free to pick my interviews
when and where I want to have them.
Stephen Harper, Prime Minister of Canada

The Prime Minister and his Cabinet Ministers held their first unpublicized and private meeting on Parliament Hill, much to the frustration of the media who felt that it was the public's right to know the plans of the government. Mr. Harper felt that, according to the Canadian Constitution, his private Cabinet meetings were justifiable and legal. His Ministers naturally were unavailable to the press after the meeting.

One of Mr. Harper's priorities is to control the message to Canadians. Ultimately, Canadians will lose if the press, the watchdog of our democracy, cannot ask questions that would either substantiate, repudiate or at least earmark the government's messages for closer scrutiny.

His strategy is understandable in light of the Conservatives' loss in the previous election. Harper, a quick learner, realized that to be successful, he needed to muzzle his underlings and tightly control the Party message. It proved to be a winning decision. It doesn't change the fact that "rogue" thoughts and views exist amongst his caucus. Even now, they occasionally pop out (Garth Turner and Michael Chong - Long live integrity!). It's just so much nicer for the Tories when Canadians don't have to hear them.

Thus, the autocratic control by the PMO and the almost perfect illusion of solidarity continues. During Question Period, one hears frequent shouts of "Here, here!" from the government side, but one wonders about the thoughts that may lurk behind the many expressionless faces of Harper's foot soldiers.

Once Upon a Dumpster

The gulls and a stray cat were surprised this morning,
As they pecked and scratched for daily fare,
A sleek, black limousine approached sans warning.
And stopped alongside their dumpster there.

The scavengers stood steadfast to guard their treasure,
As guards jumped out and scanned the way.
Looking carefully over their shoulders for good measure,
Stephen was keeping the press at bay.

The PM smirked and hustled smartly through the rear door,
The "insurgent press" waited out front.
"Why fear us? We stand for truth, we are the press corps!
Your secret meetings are an affront!"

The third floor was safe, the bunkers were securely manned.
The Cabinet met and their leader spoke,
"When you leave, conversation with the press is banned.
Hear my words now, this is not a joke!"

"Aye, aye, Captain!" they robotically chanted,
The press cried, "Give us information!"
Their fearless leader remained steadfast and undaunted,
While he hid behind the Constitution.

The gulls and the stray cat continued to forage,
Wond'ring about their a.m. surprise.
They had trouble processing the P.M.'s garbage,
So left it for the scavenging flies.

With the opening of Parliament, ghostlike images of new Cabinet Ministers and their fellow Conservative MPs morphed into flesh and blood as they filed into the House of Commons. The only thing missing during their debut was a long rope that would have safely bound them together.

Stephen Harper's gag order had made them extremely furtive and very skittish, fearful of inadvertently running into the press. Notable amongst them was David Emerson, who, almost before the ballots had a chance to cool from the counting, had brazenly disenfranchised the Liberal voters of his Vancouver-Kingsway riding. In protest, an angered constituent hired a plane to fly over Parliament Hill, visually expressing his frustration.

The Coming Out Party

The 39th Parliament opened today,
Harper's kids were scrubbed and ready to play.
"No longer in hiding, not docile and meek,
d'ya think Papa Harper will now let us speak?

We are wishing, wishing, with all of our might,
that Daddy will trust us and let us take flight.
We promise, we promise, we'll really be nice,
before speaking out, we will get your advice!"

The bad boy on the block was cocky and sure,
hoping space and time his defection would cure.
Gazing skyward to read, his mouth it did foam,
the banner read, "David Emerson call home!"

The P.M. was witty and very secure,
his motives were noble, his heart, it was pure!
He'd mold this country and would never lament,
to hell with ethics and transparent.

The former Liberal cabinet minister David Emerson, who crossed the floor to the Conservatives shortly after being re-elected, continued to be dogged by his constituents from Vancouver-Kingsway.

In response to this situation, Mr. Emerson commented, "… every once in a while the locusts descend on me and it creates situations that are a little abnormal, but I carry on with my work."[1] In response to continued protest, this time in Burnaby, B.C., Prime Minister Harper belittled the continued outrage over this strike against democracy, stating that it's "...the same 10 people every time. You know, it's kind of getting old hat, isn't it?"[2]

Over 32,000 Liberal and NDP voters were essentially disen-franchised by Harper's sacrifice of democracy for the sake of better representation for B.C. This smells like a rotten salmon and no one would ever swallow that.

Locusts, You Say?

Ten little locusts, protesting on the Hill,
CSIS slipped one a cyanide pill.
Stevie called the spin doctor,
the spin doctor said,
"Before much longer,
nine more will be dead!"

Nine little locusts, criticizing Stephen,
"Hey, little locusts, now I'll get even!"
Stevie called the spin doctor,
the spin doctor said,
"Before much longer,
eight more will be dead!"

Eight little locusts, sitting in protest,
Called the police, rid of one more pest,
Stevie called the spin doctor,
the spin doctor said,
"Before much longer,
seven more will be dead!"

Seven little locusts, making such a flap,
"All over nothing, I'll give you such a slap!"
Stevie called the spin doctor,
the spin doctor said,
"Before much longer,
six more will be dead!"

Six little locusts, calling for a vote,
"For that silliness, one more I will smote!"
Stevie called the spin doctor,
the spin doctor said,
"Before much longer,
five more will be dead!"

Five little locusts, demanding their rights,
"Get off of our backs, you're right in our sights!"
Stevie called the spin doctor,
the spin doctor said,
"Before much longer,
four more will be dead!"

Four little locusts, planting flags on the Hill.
"Where do you get off? Just one more we will kill!"
Stevie called the spin doctor,
the spin doctor said,
"Before much longer,
three more will be dead!"

Three little locusts, disdaining the plot.
"We pilfered your votes? Vile insects we'll swat!"
Stevie called the spin doctor,
the spin doctor said,
"Before much longer,
two more will be dead!"

Two little locusts, breathing greenhouse air,
one tumbled to earth, dying of despair.
Stevie called the spin doctor,
the spin doctor said,
"Before much longer,
one more will be dead!"

One little locust, pleading for ethics.
Democracy lost, sure suffered its licks.
The spin doctor called Stephen,
and Stephen sat pat.
"All this complaining is simply old hat!"

111

Canadians were shocked when former Liberal Cabinet Minister David Emerson accepted Stephen Harper's invitation to join the Conservative Party shortly after his re-election as a Liberal in the Vancouver-Kingsway riding. Emerson was rewarded with a Cabinet position, a post considerably more lucrative and influential than that of a "mere" member of the Opposition.

Liberal supporters and fundraisers in Emerson's riding were outraged by what they deemed to be a blatantly unethical act by the new Prime Minister and Emerson, particularly in light of the Conservatives' major election platform that condemned corruption and a breakdown of ethics in government. Several betrayed constituents refused to leave Emerson's office when denied a meeting with the new Minister. The police were summoned and the individuals were summarily carted away in a paddy wagon. Long live democracy!

Of Ethics and Men

There once was a big L Liberal from B.C.
Who said, "I'll fight those rotten Tories, trust in me!"
But when the votes were counted,
Emerson was undaunted,
"A big C Conservative I will always be!"

Stephen Harper offered him some very yummy bait,
He swore it was for British Columbia's sake!
"You cannot have your vote back,
Now please don't overreact,
You'd almost think that democracy was at stake!"

David Emerson slipped neatly into hiding,
From the angry, riled up voters of his riding.
"Please explain to us at least.
Oh, oh, here come the police!
You call this transparency? We're sure not buying!"

Since their minority victory on January 23, the Conservative Party, under the direction and very tight control of the Prime Minister, became elusive to the press in direct contradiction of their platform that had called for accountability and transparency. In spite of this promise, all communication from Conservative MPs and senior officials had to first be approved by the Prime Minister unless it specifically related to the Conservatives' five-point plan for the country. The Parliamentary Press, consequently, found it extremely difficult to access information from the new government.

The Prime Minister had slowly become selective about his availability to reporters. In April of 2006, after announcing the Accountability Act, national television audiences enjoyed an impromptu slapstick comedy routine when the PM subsequently met with the Parliamentary Press. Harper had designated a reporter to ask a question, but Julie Van Dusen of CBC's *The National* insisted that she was at the front of the line to ask questions and continually interrupted him, asking him why he was ignoring the line-up of reporters for those he chose to answer. The Prime Minister tried to ignore her, called on another reporter on five separate occasions to ask a question, then finally, in a rare instance of giving in, he gave up in frustration and allowed the CBC reporter to pose her question! The ability of the press to inform the Canadian people about the workings of the government has become seriously imperiled.

The Truth Shall Make You Free

The future of democracy oft becomes tenuous,
when a leader's actions veer towards the ingenuous.
For the most sacred trust is the elected right to rule,
respected by a sage and ignored by a fool.

The opinion of voters gives the government power,
elected members try but can't hide in ivory towers.
Directness and transparency need their proper address,
the ears of the people are the Parliamentary Press.

When forces against democracy take over a land,
leaders often muzzle the press as quickly as they can.
But knowledge permits casting of an intelligent vote,
that allows only the best government to stay afloat.

O Canada, we fear for thee.

The Cabinet meets, Ministers no longer face the press,
what is happening here, why do we deserve so much less?
All MPs communication screened by the PMO,
tightly controlled party lines to the public will flow.

Keen watchdog opposition at Public Works can't bay,
within the Senate Chamber, Michael Fortier's cached away.
The press may question Ambrose on her environmental task,
conditional that questions on Kyoto they don't ask.

Excluding promises for much more accessibility,
Harper presented his bill on accountability.
More freedom of information he elected to defer,
for less government scrutiny we can only infer.

Where's the elusive transparency he spoke of aloud?
After pledging it so often, voters finally bowed.
Fearful of repercussions when he met up with the press,
he told them straightaway you will have two questions at best

The people's right to know is crucial for democracy,
to ensure accountability and transparency.
To abide by the Scriptures, journalists our eyes must be,
    and then shall you know the truth,
      and the truth shall make you free.

During Stephen Harper's first 100 days as Prime Minister, he often demonstrated a blatant disrespect of democratic process, from his anger over his unsuccessful attempt to appoint Gwyn Morgan to lead the new Public Appointments Commission to his blatant disregard of true parliamentary process in the Afghanistan vote.

Mr. Morgan, a Conservative fundraiser, Liberal basher and former high profile CEO of an Alberta oil company who vehemently opposed Kyoto, seemed an unlikely candidate for a position designed to ensure the elimination of partisan appointments. In a tantrum-like response to a parliamentary committee's initiative to remove Morgan as their chairperson, an angered Harper announced that he would kill his proposal for a Public Appointments' Commission, a key component of his promised accountability package.

With respect to Harper's wish to extend the Afghanistan mission for two years, MPs were disgusted with Harper's tactics. He announced that parliament would have a vote on this proposal with only a thirty-six hour warning followed by a six-hour debate. As a preface to the debate, Harper stated that if he did not receive a majority vote, he would extend the mission by one year anyway, then go to the Canadian people in an election for the second year.

Opposition MPs viewed his action as more bullying and a political ploy disrespectfully made on the backs of our combat troops in Afghanistan. They sought details about the terms of the extension and were frustrated when repetitively told that their questions indicated a lack of support of the troops.

It is interesting to note that the Netherlands had discussed their extension for about nine months before making their decision. Harper's behavior was viewed by many as a major slight on parliamentary and democratic process and a rejection of the wishes of Canadians.

The Vote

Across our fair land thrives a new democracy,
based on a newly developed form of Harpocrisy.
One person, one vote, is still the Canadian way,
but if you decide against him, he'll still do it his own way.

It began with Emerson, as a Liberal he had won,
his Liberal supporters, he successfully did con.
All it needed was his asking, Steve was not surprised,
the cost was minimal, only thousands disenfranchised.

In this world, all new Senators would have to be elected,
partisan style of appointments he had long since rejected.
Now that he was in power, he mustn't get carried away,
A new style of leadership, welcome Michael Fortier.

He selected Morgan for his Appointments' Commission,
partisanship would certainly go straight into remission.
A committee soon voted to relieve him of the chair,
rejecting his good Tory friend, how totally unfair!

The Afghanistan vote, how democratic could that be?
He gave six hours to decide, "Please, do go along with me."
What's the big deal? He hoped he did not appear didactic.
You can't really think this was a shrewd political tactic!

So you want answers, this will be the only one you hear,
"To ask questions is traitorous!" his minions would jeer.
If they didn't vote right, he'd play games of Harpocrisy,
He really liked this new form of stylized democracy.

Then there's the plea to keep Kyoto, what an inane joke!
Why listen to the Commons stupid majority vote?
They're all trying his patience, he's a ruler on the rise,
He promised a new Canada that no one would recognize.

Vimy Ridge, Easter Monday, April 9, 1917. Canadian soldiers, encumbered by heavy packs, fought their way through mud, high winds, treacherous terrain and sleet and snow to face German soldiers and their firmly entrenched machine guns. 3,598 Canadian soldiers out of 10,602 casualties gave their lives, all courageously fighting for freedom and democracy. Brigadier-General Alexander Ross, commander of the 28th Battalion at Vimy Ridge, stated, "It was Canada from the Atlantic to the Pacific on parade. I thought then... that in those few minutes I witnessed the birth of a nation."[3]

Prime Minister Harper, while touring this historic and very sacred World War I battlefield during his international G-8 visit, chose this time to criticize the press. It was a very unfitting choice of venue to slam the free press, an absolutely necessary component of the true democracy that so many Canadians fought and died for.

Vimy Ridge Revisited

With raw valour and tightly controlled fear, their hearts pounding,
our soldiers slogged through the spring mud, adrenaline pumping, rippling
in blood waves, nerves jagged, firing within their spines,
as they advanced or fell confronting the enemy lines.

Their blood lies in communion with the consecrated earth,
that interred Canada's fallen leaves, then marking the birth
of an independent nation that answered freedom's call.
The wind whispers their names through the open-air cathedral.

Four Victorian Crosses won there the very first day,
thousands dead, many more wounded in this deadly foray.
A tribute to our country's resolve, set to pay the price,
offering her native sons' lives, the final sacrifice.

Our Prime Minister, there to honour this most sacred site,
chose his words shrewdly, raised him to unprecedented height,
"And the enemies used guns, not a camera," he quipped,
While smirking at the press, he used Vimy for one more lick.

Stephen's at it again. With an almost obsessive desire to break with tradition and impose personal ideology, he has once again compromised democratic process. The latest front line is in the Prairies where the majority of farmers have come to prefer and depend on the Canada Wheat Board to sell their crops. Harper made an election promise that he would scrap the Board once he was elected, and - surprise, surprise - he has decisively bumbled his way forward to keep his word at whatever the cost.

Since the Board's inception in the 1920s, it has evolved into an efficient mechanism that sells wheat and barley in Canada and throughout the rest of the world, guaranteeing security and a good return on the crops. Majority of Western farmers want the status quo and are outraged by the long hand of the government interfering with their livelihood.

The question of relevance of the Board is not even the issue. By law, the farmers have the right of a plebiscite to determine their wishes. Harper has used the divide-and-conquer approach to get his way. After much controversy, he decided to finally allow a vote, but only from the barley growers. There is great concern that the government will alter the list of eligible voters to obtain the desired result.

The PM undoubtedly feels confident that if the barley growers agree, which is questionable, then the precedent would be set for the next attack, which would be against the wheat growers. He gagged the president of the Board, Adrian Measner, from publicly presenting the positive side of continuing with the Board. When Measner's professionalism and loyalty to farmers prevailed and he spoke out, Harper fired him. This isn't the first time he has given the pink slip to someone who dared to disagree with him. Former Conservative MP Garth Turner also felt the edge of the PM's sword.

A previous Conservative government, that of Arthur Meighen, abolished the Wheat Board in the early 20s and the consequent backlash contributed to the defeat of his government. Why, then, would Harper risk a similar fate when his popularity has been slipping? No one knows the answer for certain; however, the U.S. would be ecstatic over the Wheat Board's demise. Their trade challenges against the Board have been unfruitful to date. Is this nothing but another concession Harper is willing to give the United States as part of his cozy-up-to-George-Bush strategy? Isn't democratic process and freedom of expression more in line with the Canada we know? Canada is a nation distinct and separate from the U.S. Canadians value this tradition and would be loathe seeing it destroyed.

Corn Bob Sees the Light of Day

Corn Bob rolled monotonously on his trusty creaky ol' rocker,
At his feet, his faithful hound, who weren't never much of a talker.
"Harpo, my boy," he said to it in a quiet confidante tone,
"Fetch me mah slippers and I'll go git ya a fresh, juicy cow bone."

An hour had barely passed when ol' Harpo commenced a barkin',
And Bob looked out the window to see a black SUV a parkin'.
"Betty-Jo, throw on the coffee pot, it's Steve, mah first cuzzin!"
His wife dropped her chores and in the kitchen started a fussin'.

With a blast of wind the door whipped open and there stood cuzzin' Steve,
That hound dog whimpered softly and laid himself down with a heave.
Bob and Steve then shook hands lookin' just a bit mite too formal,
Something thick hung in the air, these two weren't actin' normal.

"Set yourself down afore the woodstove and help get ridda that chill.
So how are things a farin' on that parliamentary hill?"
Cuzzin' Steve just sat there as his energy was mighty fizzled,
And spat a heavy on the stove and watched as it did sizzle.

"Well Bob," he said, "when we began we was kickin' like young foals,
We gave it our best shot, but gawd we tumbled down in the polls!
My heart is warm and cozy, sure don't mean nobody no harm,
Can't figgur out why they're soundin' that darn ol' election alarm."

Words were barely spoken before a stink lifted from the floor,
Bob jumped up and retched and gasped and kicked open the front door.
Steve turned green and asked his cuzzin' what had made that abominable
stink.
"Oh," he answered, "That's just ol' Harpo telling you he don't like what you
think."

Once the air had cleared, the Misses brought them in coffee and cake,
Long ago Bob had proposed when he had seen how well she could bake.
Without a word, she served the men, her eyes turned towards the floor,
And Steve complimented Bob on "A true fine woman! Who needs more!"

The plaisant'ries over, the cuzzins kicked back and each lit up a fag,
It weren't too long before there was a conversational lag.
Bob cleared his throat and wet his lips and finally broke the ice,
"I gotta talk with you, cuzzin' Steve, about sumthin' not too nice."

"Now me and the boys was a talkin' the other day down at that general store,
What you and your friend Chuckie did sure did rile us up to the core.
Takin' away the right to vote as one is mighty brassy,
Then firin' the farmers' man, now cuzzin' Steve, that's downright sassy!"

"Mah good buddies are cheesed like two ol' roosters in a hen coop,
They're all a scratchin' and a fightin' cuz ya threw them for a loop.
Can ya tell me why you're makin' all this dangamit trouble?
Forgive me for askin' cuz I sure don't wanna burst your bubble."

"Well ya see Bob, I think farmers they should have the right to choose.
Sorry for puttin' it that way, you know those words I seldom use.
Ya know I fight hard to protect all these democratic rights."
Then another smell in the room rose to unprecedented heights.

"Steve, Harpo and me know it's the Yanks that you's wantin' t' please,
It's ol' Bush and his grain growers you're aimin' hard to appease!
If ya can't tell me straight, reckon you'd best be moseying along!"
And as sure as rain within seconds, cuzzin' Steve was sure as gone.

The premature retirement of Jean-Pierre Kingsley, Canada's Chief Electoral Officer, came as a shock. Although Kingsley was profusely praised by the Prime Minister shortly after the announcement, Harper has had a long-standing dispute with the man. This raised a very healthy dose of speculation that the Conservatives' actions had pressured him to leave his office.

As a former president of the National Citizens' Coalition, the PM vehemently criticized Kingsley when he enforced a law against publicizing federal election results prior to the closure of all polling stations in Canada. In fact, he helped in the process of soliciting money to assist the offender. To some, Harper is a man who appears to lack understanding about what it takes to safeguard democracy. He also laid into the Chief Electoral Officer for his restriction of election advertisement by non-Party groups. As Canadian Alliance leader, he was distressed that Kingsley had charged Party members for anonymously publishing a poll that they themselves had conducted, again contrary to the Election Act. The Prime Minister has used extremely colourful words to describe a man of such high calibre and accomplishments.

Recently, Kingsley raised ire and fire when he stated that the Conservatives failed to declare their national convention fees in 2005 as political donations. He was then displeased that the Tories balked at his request to see their convention books. After Harper's failure to legalize their past action through the modification of the Accountability Act, he finally authorized revisions and resubmission of their financial report to Elections Canada. This quietly transpired during the Christmas break.

The Conservatives didn't declare hundreds of thousands of dollars of convention donations and, taking it directly to the top, the Prime Minister himself had exceeded the legal amount for a personal donation. The extra money, which contravened the Election Act, gave the Conservatives an unfair advantage during their campaign and may have played a significant role in their election to office. The Conservatives had offered their squeaky clean approach to governance to the Canadian people.

Through a Glass House Darkly

Jean-Pierre Kingsley, that strong democratic overseer,
stood steadfastly against Harper and his misguided fears.
Riled by Election Canada, Steve launched a mean attack,
Kingsley, indignant and stunned, was completely taken aback.

In B.C. a man charged, it was a breach of the Election Act,
the law openly broken, it was an irrefutable fact.
Posted a voter outcome, brought early news to the west,
Such an extreme contravention cried out to be addressed.

Steve backed the offender, fell into a spiraling roll.
The "jackasses" at Election Can were out of control.

Two Ontario workers charged, had placed a newspaper ad,
published their own poll results and the public had been had.
Didn't give Elections Can details of their research,
democracy once again left far behind in the lurch.

Stephen fumed and exploded, engulfed in indignant rage,
tagged Kingsley's decisive action as nothing but "garbage."

A recent war update had flashed to all parts of the nation,
based on the rules that covered all political donation.
Kingsley called for the Tory's books and met with much resistance,
Harper had moved quickly into a full stance defensive.

Words echoed from before, "dangerous and heavy handed,
state policeman, Electoral Nanny," Kingsley had been branded.

A stalemate existed and there emerged a resolution,
Baird failed to change the accountability legislation.
Hope shattered, Harper authorized his report's revision,
the numbers were staggering, gave voters a clear vision.

Donations went far beyond the Election Canada ceiling,
an unfair campaign advantage and questionable dealing.
Transparency and accountability both tossed aside,
when living in a glass house, there is nothing you can hide.

Near the end of the 2005/2006 election campaign, RCMP Commissioner Giuliano Zaccardelli sent a personally signed letter to NDP MP Judy Wasylycia-Leis stating that he would be conducting a criminal investigation into an alleged wrongdoing that led to insider trading on Bay Street.[4]

At the centre of the controversy was Ralph Goodale, the Liberal Finance Minister at that time, who, it was alleged, tipped off investors about a tax policy change re: income trusts. This news flashed through the media and shortly thereafter, the polls dipped six points for the Liberals and they suddenly trailed the Conservatives. The Tories incorporated the allegation into their intense advertising campaign on "Liberal corruption."

Zaccardelli's decision to make public his intent without substantive evidence tipped the scales in favour of the Tories. One year later, the RCMP inquiry had produced no proof that Goodale and the Liberals had behaved inappropriately, yet the government continued to suggest wrongdoing during Question Period in the Commons. The reputation of a highly principled man remained tarnished. Unproven allegations have no place in a democratic election or in the daily operation of Parliament.

Zaccardelli was again in the news recently when he changed the first testimony he had made to the Commons committee handling the Arar investigation. Surprisingly, the Prime Minister and Public Safety Minister Day placed their unequivocal public support behind the commissioner until after his second testimony and his subsequent resignation. The question remains as to whether or not Minister Day had advised the Prime Minister several months before the new disclosure to remove Zaccardelli from his post. A direct answer from Day was not forthcoming when MP Mark Holland repeatedly asked this question during a committee meeting. If the answer was yes, why did the PM and Day continue to publicly support the commissioner without hesitation? Answers to such important questions should never be left outstanding.

Tread Carefully

With democracy, due diligence is standard fare,
to preserve freedom and individual right.
Forthrightness and truth demonstrate we honestly care,
that ethics and principles are stronger than might.
Poor judgment or luck or even misguided concern,
shouldn't interfere with a nation's daily life.
The overpowering wants of but a few, we must learn,
shall only bring about unwanted turmoil and strife.
A lesson for the learning for all politicians,
regardless of party or one's personal aim.
Honest integrity surpasses all ambitions,
one's moral action surpasses all short term gain.

ENDNOTES

1. "Emerson granted rare protest-free appearance." Canada.com. 16 April, 2006. <http://www.canada.com/topics/news/politics/story. html?id=864df870-610f-4154-a9ee-e875509eb5b9&k=95646>

2. Whittington, Les. "Emerson frustrated, ex-aide says 'Tories too partisan.'" The Toronto Star. 20 April 2006.

3. Masse, Martin. "Vimy Ridge: Can a War Massacre Give Birth to a Nation?" Editorial, Quebecoislibre.org, 13 April 2002. <http://www.quebecoislibre.org/020413-2.htm>

4. "Liberals say they should have fired Zaccardelli during election campaign." Canada.com. 07 December 2006. <http://www.canada.com/ottawacitizen/story.html?id=db567c01-1676-4efc-b730-b242ef54ec49>

Old Clothes

Before too long, cruel changes had been made,
The peasants grew poorer, their hopes began to fade.
Knights walked boldly, obeyed ev'ry command,
Wreaked total havoc throughout this peace-loving land.

The light of democracy had soon grew dim,
Traditions had fallen to ideological whim.
Social justice was nothing but a thought from the past,
Most wondered how long this abandonment would last.

Subjects seemed restless with each passing hour,
They opposed the abuse of a king's absolute power.
They yearned for that time when the heart, it had ruled,
And felt ashamed that they had been so easily fooled.

One day the king strode high into the market place,
Wearing the opulent cloth that had marked his high place.
Among them, a young boy howled, "He ain't got nothing on!"
The king's armor had a chink and his disguise was then gone.

The crowd roared with laughter and some sighed with joy,
Through a child's innocent eyes they had seen the king's ploy.
Knowledge is power and to question a must,
A monarch with wants hidden, you must learn to never trust.

Dazed and confused, the king cut and he ran,
Summoned his counselors, frantic for a new plan.
His subjects much wiser, no longer naïve,
They'd be harder to fool and less likely to believe.

About the Author

Walter Belsito resides in rural Northern Ontario near Sault Ste Marie where he was born and raised. He was briefly a news reporter/announcer at a local television radio station in the Sault and has had a longstanding interest in Canadian politics.

He served as a teacher with CUSO (Canadian University Service Overseas) in a remote region of Papua, New Guinea, where his wife Lynda, the other half of the volunteer team, worked as a hospital and community nurse. Walter later taught in Northern Manitoba and in Northern Ontario, where he eventually became a principal.

He immensely enjoys the creative process and appreciates the value and power of the written word. Other than writing, his interests include a love of Nature and photography, sketching, painting and playing the guitar. Walter and Lynda have three grown children and three grandchildren.

About the Illustrator

Josh Beutel is a Saint John, New Brunswick-based cartoonist. For the past 34 years he has produced editorial cartoons on a contract and freelance basis for weekly and daily newspapers in Canada. His work has been mostly associated with the New Brunswick *Telegraph-Journal* where he has worked for twenty years. He has produced 5 books of his cartoons, the last being *True Blue Grit: A Frank McKenna Review.*